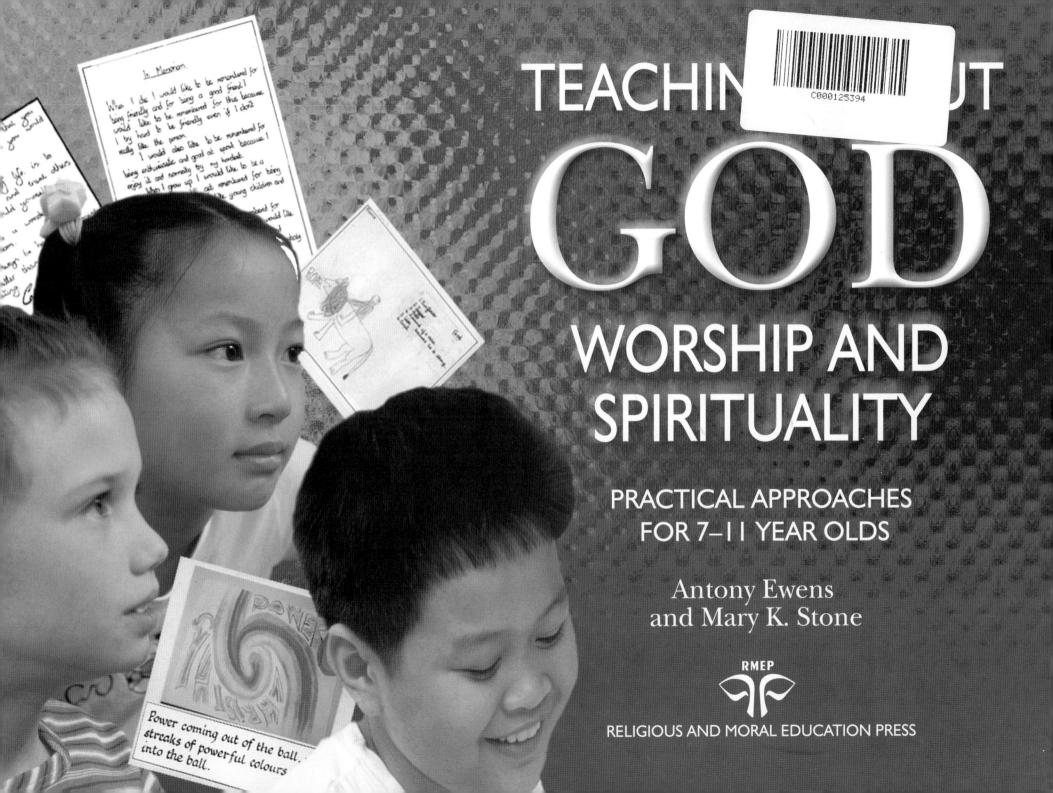

TEACHING ABOUT GOD
WORSHIP AND SPIRITUALITY

PRACTICAL APPROACHES FOR 7–11 YEAR OLDS

Antony Ewens
and Mary K. Stone

RMEP

RELIGIOUS AND MORAL EDUCATION PRESS

Religious and Moral Education Press
A division of SCM-Canterbury Press Ltd
A wholly owned subsidiary of Hymns Ancient & Modern Ltd
St Mary's Works, St Mary's Plain
Norwich, Norfolk NR3 3BH

First published 2001

ISBN 1 85175 224 2

About the Authors

Mary Stone and Tony Ewens teach RE at St Martin's College, Lancaster, where they have contributed to both pre-service and in-service courses. They are both experienced primary-school teachers who have held headships and been RE co-ordinators, and both have worked as advisory teachers for RE, in Cumbria and Devon respectively.

Acknowledgements

We should like to acknowledge our gratitude to the following who have helped us in a variety of ways in the preparation of this book:

Staff and pupils of Sedbergh Primary School, Cumbria, and especially Jan McArthur, St Mark's School, Natland, Cumbria, the governors of Hornby CE Primary School, Lancashire and Oldham LEAs.

Designed and typeset by TOPICS – The Creative Partnership, Exeter
Illustrations mostly come from Sedbergh Primary School
Cover photographs: Digital Imagery © copyright 2001 Photodisc, Inc.
Printed in Great Britain by David Gregson Associates, Beccles, Sulfolk, for SCM-Canterbury Press Ltd, Norwich.

Preface

We have written this book in order to share with other teachers some practical ideas on RE with pupils in the 7–11 age group. The approaches that we describe have been used in classrooms, with positive results for children's motivation and learning. They spring from a determination to link children's growing knowledge about religion with developing their ability to reflect on their own ideas, opinions and beliefs.

Above all, this material is designed to be a source of ideas. We hope that teachers will draw on our examples by amending and adapting them to suit the needs of their pupils. The content and the methods which we describe are congruent with current statutory syllabuses for RE.

At the beginning of each piece of work an age range is given. This indicates the ages of the particular group of children whose responses are included in that example. It does not mean that the topic is suitable only for that age group. Many of these examples can be adapted to suit any children aged between 7 and 11 years, or indeed, older children, and the same basic content has been used with adults as well, e.g. with teachers on in-service courses.

We dedicate this book to our colleague Lorna Crossman, Senior Lecturer in Primary RE at St Martin's College, with thanks for the many insights she has shared with us.

Contents

The Starting-Point

Every subject in the primary school curriculum has changed significantly in the last half century, but perhaps none more so than Religious Education. Differences in the religious, cultural and moral make-up of the community and a profound change in attitude towards the place of religion in society have brought about a re-evaluation of the place and scope of RE as an educational activity. This has been widely debated in journals and its implications have been extensively considered by each Local Education Authority (LEA) in England and Wales as it has written and reviewed its Agreed Syllabus for RE. However, as OFSTED reports often demonstrate, the practical applications of the change in thinking about RE have been slow to percolate into classrooms. This is hardly surprising, given the phenomenal demands made upon primary teachers by a constantly evolving national curriculum, the national literacy and numeracy strategies, statutory assessment, recording and reporting of pupils' attainment and the rapid development of new technology. RE is but one demand among many.

Despite official encouragement to introduce more subject-specialist teaching for ages 7–11, most primary practioners are still predominantly class teachers, attempting to provide the full range of a broad and balanced curriculum for their classes. In RE this is a mixed blessing. On one hand it means that children are tackling RE with a teacher who will know each of them very well, and this can be a major benefit to their spiritual, moral, social and cultural development. On the other hand the majority of primary teachers have only a limited knowledge of the key features of the principal faiths covered in contemporary syllabuses. Many of them will have experienced RE in their own schooldays restricted to the telling and learning of biblical stories, and the few hours devoted to RE in their teacher training will have done little to equip them with more than a sketchy outline of the subject knowledge which seems to be taken for granted by today's syllabus makers.

Getting Started

It is our view that the most important task in RE at ages 7–11 is to help pupils to forge a link between their own spiritual development and the ideas, practices and teachings of the faiths about which they learn. By pupils' spiritual development we mean their capacity to reflect on what it means to be a human being, with emotions and insights as well as thoughts and knowledge, and their ability to explore big questions about the origins, purpose and end of life, the nature of human relationships and the relationship between human beings and their environment. These issues form a key part of the agendas of each of the principal religions. By encountering examples of the ways in which some people have answered – and continue to answer – the big questions about human existence, children can be helped to shape and formulate their own responses and views.

In order to bring this aspiration to life in the primary classroom, teachers of RE need:

- to see RE as open and exploratory, and be willing to explore their own beliefs and values;

- to view their own role as that of educator rather than instructor;

- to help children to engage in a quest for meaning and purpose in life.

What follows in this book is founded on these principles.

A Practical Approach to Religious Education

In our work with teachers, on both pre-service and in-service courses, the commonest request that we receive is:

> *Give us some practical ideas for RE that we can use in the classroom.*

We are happy to oblige (see pages 16–63). But even the best of practical ideas depends to some extent for its success upon the teacher's knowledge and understanding of the subject-matter and appreciation of the aims and purposes of the subject. No amount of practical advice can equip you to handle the unexpected, spontaneous question from a pupil or parent (or, perish the thought, OFSTED inspector).

- So our first practical advice is that there is no substitute for thinking through your understanding of the role of RE in the school curriculum.

- Our second suggestion is that you should develop gradually your knowledge of the religions covered in the syllabus that you are required to teach.

- A third recommendation is that you review the range of teaching and learning styles that you use in RE.

However, we do not hold to the view that you need a full grasp of theory before you can begin with practice. The relationship between practice and theory is much more complex than that. We have both developed much of our theoretical understanding of RE through reflecting on our work in classrooms, in primary schools and in pre-service and in-service work with teachers in a college and for several LEAs. We also acknowledge our indebtedness to many authors of books about RE. But we have derived the greatest benefit from books and journals through having already tackled aspects of the subject in a practical way. We find ourselves recognizing the ideas and issues dealt with in the literature because we have already encountered them in the classroom. The writers then help us to evaluate our practice, to build on the strengths and eliminate the weaknesses. Our recommended approach is precisely the same as that followed by Early Years pupils whose teachers use the High/Scope method:

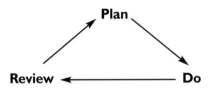

Constant use of this cycle leads to the ongoing development and refinement of a theoretical approach to RE by a process of reflection on practice. But your theories never become divorced from reality because they immediately feed back into the classroom through your next plans.

The most important stage of the cycle is the review. This may comprise some or all of the following:

- evaluation – of processes and/or outcomes;
- reflection – on what has been achieved, and what might follow;
- discussion – with colleagues and/or pupils;
- reading – RE scheme or syllabus, journal or books.

However, you cannot review an RE lesson until you have taught one. The activities in this book are designed as 'starters', to be used with or without adaptation, to get you under way in the cycle of Plan–Do–Review.

This is emphatically **not** a volume of ideas to be used unthinkingly. We encourage you to modify and amend our work, in particular to meet the needs of the children you teach. Above all, we want to offer as starting-points ideas that have been tried out in classrooms, and which worked. They are presented as a means to an end: as

launching-pads to provide teachers with the confidence to develop their own repertoire of approaches through engaging in the cycle of Plan–Do–Review which we have found so beneficial.

The Questions People Ask

This section deals with some of the questions that class teachers in England and Wales most frequently ask us about RE. We mention them here for two reasons:

- to provide some answers;
- to equip RE co-ordinators who will no doubt encounter the same questions.

Is RE in the National Curriculum?

Yes and no! RE is part of the basic curriculum, required by law to be taught in all maintained schools in England and Wales. The Dearing Review of the National Curriculum recommended that it be allocated at least 45 hours per year at Key Stage 2 and 36 hours at Key Stage 1. When the Labour government lifted the requirement to teach the full programmes of study in the foundation subjects (Art, Design & Technology, Geography, History, Music and PE), the Secretary of State made it clear that no reduction in RE was permitted. RE is therefore classified as one of the core subjects, along with English, Mathematics, Science and ICT, and OFSTED has instructed its inspectors to inspect it as such. However, there is no national programme of study for RE. The QCA programmes of study show possible ways of planning schemes of work, though teachers will need to be careful that any adopted fulfil the requirements of their own Agreed Syllabus. The QCA *Non-statutory guidance on RE* (ref. QCA/00/576) is an excellent guide to all planning.

Why is there no national programme of study for RE?

Two main reasons: first, before the National Curriculum came in there was already a procedure in place for agreeing syllabuses for RE, and this has continued, and secondly, the dual system of schools includes denominational schools, some of which have the authority to give religious education in accordance with the faith to which they belong.

How do I know which syllabus to use?

Community schools and almost all foundation schools use the agreed syllabus of their LEA. This is agreed by the LEA on the advice of a conference (called a SACRE) including representatives of the Church of England, other Christian denominations, other principal faiths with a significant local presence, the teaching profession and elected councillors. It must be non-denominational in character and must reflect the major role of Christianity within national culture but also require teaching about the other principal faiths practised in Britain (defined usually as Buddhism, Hinduism, Islam, Judaism and Sikhism).

Almost all aided schools have a denominational character (Church of England and Roman Catholic are the most numerous, and there are also Methodist, Jewish and Islamic schools). The governors of these schools are responsible for ensuring that the character of RE is in accordance with the traditions of their foundation. In practice the governors usually adopt a syllabus proposed by their religious authorities. Teaching about that particular religious tradition will be prominent, but most syllabuses used in aided schools also require teaching about other faiths and denominations.

In most schools the RE co-ordinator will have led the drawing up of a scheme of work which is in line with the syllabus, so other teachers should not have to become very closely involved with the syllabus itself.

Why teach RE in schools?
Surely we should educate, not indoctrinate?

With respect, you've answered your own question. Indoctrination (promoting one point of view as if there were no other) is specifically ruled out in legislation. In the syllabuses of LEAs and religious authorities alike the RE teacher is seen an educator, who helps children to explore a range of religious practices, beliefs and customs and a variety of human experiences. Against this backdrop it is for parents to arrange for their children's nurture within a religion if they wish.

What's the point of RE?

The School Curriculum and Assessment Authority (SCAA) produced in 1994 some Model Syllabuses for RE, and these have been re-issued by its successor body, the Qualifications and Curriculum Authority (QCA). These syllabuses are not addressed to schools. They are principally provided for LEAs, to guide them in making their agreed syllabuses.

The Model Syllabuses propose two attainment targets:

AT1 – Learning about religions
AT2 – Learning from religion

Many LEAs have incorporated these into their syllabuses. In others, even if they have not done so, it is possible to trace two separate strands within their documents, and we find these ATs useful in helping to achieve and maintain balance in a programme of RE.

AT1 ('Learning about religions') sets out to give children an understanding of the main practices and beliefs of the principal faiths. Given the continuing prevalence among primary teachers of the notion that concrete experiences logically precede abstract thought, it may help if you pose the question in this way:

What do Christians (or Muslims, or Jews, etc.) do and why do they do it?

Most RE syllabuses ask you to teach about a range of practices (such as worship, lifestyle, festivals, initiation ceremonies and the roles of special places and people) in Christianity and two other faiths at ages 7–11. A wider range of topics and religions is covered at ages 11–14. A secure grasp of this information and a developing understanding of the role of the various religious practices in each of the faiths is very valuable for children growing up in a plural society.

AT2 ('Learning from religion') seeks to enable children to explore their own experiences of life and to wrestle with key spiritual and moral questions: How did life begin? How will it end? Does it have a purpose or do we have to create our own meanings? How should we behave towards other people, the natural world and ourselves? Why is there suffering? What qualities and values should we admire, and which deplore? Such questions are not confined to RE; they may occur in the study of literature or science, for example. However, AT2 is always an integral part of RE. If you remove it, you are left with a 'Cook's Tour' of faiths, relying solely upon children learning and regurgitating facts about religions. Highlight AT2, however, and you engage children in the most fascinating study of all: the study of who we are and what we might be and do.

Getting to Grips with an RE Syllabus

This section is about extending your skills as an RE teacher by enhancing your understanding of the aims of the subject and thinking through the main implications of the demands of a typical RE syllabus.

Many syllabuses are based overtly on the attainment targets from the SCAA/QCA Model Syllabuses:

> *AT1 – Learning* **about** *religions*
> *AT2 – Learning* **from** *religion*

Even where this is not the case, the influence of these aspects of RE can be detected in almost all syllabuses, whether provided by LEAs or by religious authorities, in Scotland and Ireland, as well as England and Wales.

In this book we have used these two ATs to provide suggestions for learning outcomes for each of the units of work (pages 16–63). We have described them as Possible Learning Outcomes to emphasize that our ideas are open to amendment to suit the needs of particular contexts.

AT1 – Learning *about* religions

Most syllabuses describe areas of content that should be covered, arranged in a Programme of Study for each Key Stage (or even, sometimes, each year group). This content can provide a good range of general knowledge about the religions studied, and this is useful. Any teacher, however apprehensive about RE, can feel secure in dealing with factual information: Sunday is a special day for Christians, Muslims face Makkah when they pray, Jews observe the Passover each year, and so on. But if AT1 is left at that point, it is little more than a 'Trivial Pursuits' exercise in gathering snippets of information. The question 'Why?' springs readily to the lips of children aged 7–11, and in our experience the most fruitful learning in RE has often occurred when we have allowed, and even encouraged, children to pursue their 'Why?'questions.

> Why is Sunday a special day for Christians?
>
> Why do Muslims face Makkah when they pray?
>
> Why do Jews observe the Passover each year?

'Why?' is the question which points people beyond superficial knowledge towards a depth of understanding. In answering 'Why?' questions we place fragments of information into structured patterns of thinking which help us to make sense of the subject-matter.

'Why?' is also the question which arises out of curiosity and puzzlement. It is often a sign that the child who asks it has a keen motivation and interest in the topic, surely a strong enough reason to train children to adopt a questioning attitude to their learning. But 'Why?' is also the question which makes teachers of RE anxious:

> **What if I don't know the answer? …**
>
> **What if I misrepresent the deeply held beliefs of a faith community? …**
>
> **What if I don't believe it myself? …**

And it is the 'Why?' question which consequently persuades many teachers to play safe and stick to the teaching and learning of the purely factual in RE.

Here are several pertinent points that we hope will encourage you or your colleagues not to shy away from the 'Why?' questions in RE:

- There is a close connection between the 'Why' questions in AT1 in RE and the central thrust of AT1 in both Mathematics and Science. In these subjects, too, teachers are frequently less confident with open-ended, exploratory work. Inspectors often remark that mathematical investigations and scientific hypotheses and experiments are done less well than areas of Maths and Science with clear right/wrong answers. Teachers' diffidence is not due simply to the fact that RE is somehow 'different'. It has more to do with an understandable apprehension about launching into any work which cannot be planned in detail.

- The ability to sort and classify information and to place it in a structured pattern enables learners to see meaningful

7

relationships between different bits of knowledge, rather like creating a picture out of the pieces of a jigsaw. So pursuing 'Why?' questions in RE is vitally important if children are to gain a coherent view of Christianity and other religions.

- The teacher need not be the repository of all knowledge and understanding. While we don't subscribe to the 'go away and find out' response to children's awkward questions, we do believe that it is a healthy sign for teachers to reveal the limits of their own knowledge, and to express an interest in finding out what they don't know. The search for answers to 'Why?' questions readily creates realistic opportunities to use and extend higher-order English skills, whether in reading texts or electronically accessed data, or questioning a visitor from a faith community or 'interrogating' a photograph or poster.

- It is useful for children to hypothesize in RE, just as in Science. 'I wonder how many possible reasons we can think of' is a valuable precursor to some research, and children's suggestions may well provide clues as to the nature and quality of their thinking.

- Because of the diversity within religions, there may well be different 'right' answers to 'Why?' questions. Ask six Christians why they attend church and they may produce six different answers. Learning to accept and appreciate a diversity of views and beliefs is a valuable component of preparation for life in a plural society.

- If the teacher is a co-learner with the class, s/he can model appropriate attitudes of curiosity, interest, appreciation and respect, and ceases to be an apparent spokesperson for the faith being studied. S/he therefore protects the integrity of any personal religious standpoint and deals with the subject-matter in a thoroughly educational way. The use of well-briefed visitors who do represent the religions covered by the syllabus is thus doubly helpful, providing authentic data and confirming the teacher in an educator's role.

With regard to AT1 our view is, therefore, that you cannot learn about religions just by collecting factual information about them. 'What do Christians do?' is a valuable starting-point, enabling children to learn about worship, prayer, the use of the Bible, lifestyle, festivals, customs and much more. 'Why do they do it?' opens the way for an exploration of the beliefs and insights which underpin the outward manifestations of Christian practice. The same principle applies to other faiths.

AT2 – Learning *from* religion

As well as promoting knowledge and understanding of the principal faiths, RE is designed to assist children to formulate their own opinions and beliefs. 'Learning from religion' can be viewed in various ways. We consider it helpful to link this attainment target with the notions of spiritual, moral and social and cultural (SMSC) development, areas made familiar in schools in England and Wales by their inclusion in the OFSTED inspection schedule and in the QCA *Non-statutory guidance on RE* (ref. QCA/00/576).

The **spiritual** category includes feelings and insights about the purpose and meaning of life, a sense of mystery and wonder about the natural world, and ideas and beliefs about the existence of a God or gods. The approaches to RE which we describe below encourage children to pose and investigate questions of this kind and we find that the way in which we teach leads almost automatically to this sort of questioning.

Many of the issues encountered in RE also have implications about right and wrong, and lead into discussions of ethical principles and principled behaviour, thus fostering **moral** development. Often the issues raised are about the interrelationships among people within groups to which they belong, providing material for **social** development. Opportunities to promote **cultural** development are also plentiful: children can learn from religion about the way in which religious beliefs influence lifestyles, customs and traditions. They can also be encouraged to adopt a positive, appreciative attitude towards diversity.

The most profitable work in AT2 comes as a result of enabling children to explore their own responses to the aspects of religion being studied and to relate these to their own life experiences. This calls for specific skills and attitudes on the part of the teacher, chief among which are:

- an ability to frame genuinely open questions to promote enquiry;

- the use of phraseology which encourages reflection and an individual response (e.g. 'I wonder why …?');

- being prepared to accept and work with unexpected responses.

Current professional practice in primary education accentuates the importance of thorough planning by the teacher. Important though this is, there is a sense in which tight planning can stifle attainment in this area of RE. We suggest that teachers should take great care with the preparation of questions and other prompts which will promote reflection and deep thought. Thereafter they need to be ready to respond positively and productively to whatever children say. We have deliberately included in our examples extracts from conversations between teachers and pupils to illustrate ways of doing this – and to show the variety and depth of thinking which it is possible to stimulate in children aged 7–11.

Planning Units of Work

In responding to the main aims of RE set out in a syllabus, our usual practice when planning has been the following:

1. Identify the aspect of the programme of study which we intend to cover.

2. Clarify the intended learning outcomes in terms of AT1, i.e. what do we intend children to learn *about* religion?

3. Consider the possibilities offered by this topic for AT2, i.e. what might children learn *from* this area of religion?

4. Find an aspect of children's existing experience to use as a bridge between themselves and the material to be studied, e.g. work about a sacred text might begin or end with consideration of a book which is special to the pupil.

In this way we can ensure that our planning is rooted in the subject-matter set out in the syllabus and also that it relates to children's existing understanding.

How to Achieve Progression and Continuity in RE

The notions of progression and continuity imply that children's learning should be ordered and sequenced, both in a logical way and in its practical implementation in school. These ideas are perhaps most easily illustrated in Mathematics, where concepts such as addition and subtraction recur at regular intervals, with steadily increasing complexity, in a pattern which fits Bruner's idea of a 'spiral curriculum'. In Bruner's work it is the key concepts or big ideas of a subject which are the building blocks for continuity and progression. This helps to explain why Maths is so easy to describe under this heading, since its key concepts are easily identified as addition, subtraction, area, volume, capacity and so on.

The equivalent terms in RE are less apparent, but a little detective work reveals categories such as worship, ritual, deity, celebration and revelation. Your RE syllabus will be structured in such a way as to build upon these key ideas, to deepen and extend children's knowledge and understanding of them and to reflect the developmental needs of learners in a sequenced programme of study. Teachers need to be aware of this process at work in the syllabus, and in the school's associated scheme of work for RE, in order to point children back to previous learning in the same area and forward to subsequent work. This helps to create for children something of the broad canvas, of which individual topics are but a small part.

Consider, for example, the extract below from the Agreed Syllabus (1996) of the Oldham LEA:

Learning about Religions				Learning from Religion		
Key Stage 3 [Ages 11–14]	**Key Stage 2 [Ages 7–11]**	**Key Stage 1 [Ages 5–7]**	**Core Objectives**	**Key Stage 1 [Ages 5–7]**	**Key Stage 2 [Ages 7–11]**	**Key Stage 3 [Ages 11–14]**
Children should learn about the initiation rites of the religions studied.	Children should appreciate the significance of the elements in the birth rites of the religions studied.	Children should encounter the birth rite ceremonies in the religions studied.	**BELIEFS AND PRACTICES** Children will explore: • **belonging to a faith community**	Children should explore the sense of belonging to a community.	Children should develop an understanding of what it means to belong to a community.	Children should develop a sense of responsibility in relation to the immediate community.
So that they could, for example, describe the components of the initiation rites of the faiths studied, particularly those which convey the idea of commitment and responsibility.	So that they could, for example, describe the components of the birth rites in the religions studied, and explain their significance.	So that they could, for example, describe the main features of the ceremony in which young children are welcomed into a faith community.		So that they could, for example, talk about some of the groups to which they belong, or could belong, and what is good about them.	So that they could, for example, explain what benefits a particular community can give to an individual member, and what the individual would be expected to contribute in return.	So that they could, for example, identify issues concerning the school, home, or neighbourhood, to which personal action can make a contribution.

The Oldham chart demonstrates clearly an appropriate progression in teaching and learning in respect of both children's developing understanding of entry into membership of a religion (AT1) and their appreciation of the qualities and characteristics of communities of various kinds, and the responsibilities of those who belong to them (AT2). In preparing a scheme of work and in planning RE lessons, RE co-ordinators and class teachers would need an awareness of the contribution made by an individual lesson or sequence of lessons to the overall development of the concepts of initiation rites, commitment, community and responsibility.

The Oldham example applies to a topic which may be dealt with only two or three times in a child's primary-school career. Some elements of RE recur more frequently than this, especially those connected with religious festivals, and particularly any which are marked in some way within the school, as is often the case with Christmas, for example.

We have deliberately omitted from this book a section about Christmas, since this festival is observed – often excessively, in our view – in most schools. We do, however, want to refer to Christmas in this section, since inspection evidence records that this topic is often characterized by repetition rather than progression, and that pupils aged 10–11 sometimes undertake similar tasks to those tackled in the reception class. We recommend to teachers the exercise undertaken by the staff of a primary school in East Lancashire, who used the Year Theme structure of the Lancashire Agreed Syllabus to devise a programme for their two-form entry school with the aim of stimulating a developing understanding of Christmas as a Christian festival. Their programme is reproduced below, but they would be the first to assert that there is no substitute for undertaking the process by means of which they discussed and agreed their plans.

CHRISTMAS THEMES Developing Progression and Continuity		
YEAR	**THEME FROM LANCASHIRE SYLLABUS**	**SUGGESTIONS** (It is assumed that children will encounter the Christmas Story each year, in assembly, plays and carols)
R [Ages 4–5]	Community	**Gifts** 1. Discussion of gifts we'd like to receive. 2. What gifts might we give? ... to whom? why? 3. Why do people give gifts (draw out ideas that (a) this marks special occasion (b) it shows they like/love someone) 4. When using Christmas Story, emphasise the point that Jesus' birth was announced as a gift ... to Mary, to Shepherds ... and that the Kings brought gifts. What would you have taken? ... and why?
Year 1 [Ages 5–6]	God	**Births and Birthdays** 1. Discussion of the impact on a family of the arrival of a baby (practical issues and feelings, e.g. excitement, pride, jealousy). 2. What is your birthday (anniversary of your birth), how is it celebrated (bring in cards, presents, gather together for parties, sing Happy Birthday, special food, candles) 3. Why do people celebrate each other's birthdays? (Means, "you're important"). 4. When using Christmas Story, emphasise Christmas as the Christian celebration of Jesus' birthday. All the elements (cards, gifts, gatherings, food, singing [carols]) are present.
Year 2 [Ages 6–7]	Worship	**Good News** 1. Discussion of examples of good news in school or in papers/on TV. 2. How do people react to good news? (Applause, send someone a congratulations card, tell someone else about it.) 3. You could introduce the idea that sometimes people don't like hearing good news (e.g. jealous because someone else is praised). 4. When using Christmas Story, emphasise the giving of news (e.g. by the angels, and by the star, and [to Herod] by the wise men). How did people react? e.g. Shepherds, Kings went to see and take gifts. What about Herod? 5. Contemporary reactions to Christmas news: presents, parties, plays, carol singing.

Year 3 [Ages 7–8]	Founders and Leaders	**Changes** – One point about leaders is that they bring about changes in the lives of other people.

Changes – One point about leaders is that they bring about changes in the lives of other people.

1. Focus on the characters in the Christmas Story whose lives were changed. Mary and Joseph, Shepherds, Wise Men (and Herod? – threatened by change). What were the changes?
2. Identify what would be different about life in Britain if Christmas did not exist – makes point that Jesus influences everyone not just Christians.
3. How did people in the Christmas Story show how they responded to Jesus as a "leader" (e.g. Shepherds worshipped; Wise Men gave gifts; Herod tried to kill him).
4. Does the Christmas Story help you to think about changes you want or ought to make in your life (link to New Year Resolution).

Year 4 [Ages 8–9] – Living the Faith

Christmas Today – Emphasis on how Christian Churches celebrate Christmas. You might visit one to find out or collect information sheets.

1. Types of services: carols, Blessing of Crib, Midnight Mass or Communion.
2. Read some of the Bible passages used in Churches (see Y5's unit for references).
3. Look at the words of some carols. How do they link up with Bible story?
4. Charitable work – collections of money and toys for Children's Society, shelter and food for the homeless (giving as important concept in Christianity, Jesus seen as "a gift").
5. Study the Christingle ceremony, which links "giving" with the image of Jesus as "the light of the world".

Year 5 [Ages 9–10] – Sacred Books

Read All About It – Some parts of the Christmas Story are found in the Bible. Others parts are traditions, passed on orally. This unit focuses on research skill. The relevant passages are contained in Matthew chapters 1 and 2, Luke chapters 1 and 2.

1. Children give their own accounts of the Christmas Story (a list, not continuous prose).
2. Check the list against the Bible version. What's in the Bible? What's traditional?
3. Which incidents does Matthew include, but not Luke and vice versa?
4. Why do you think they give different accounts? (You could compare versions of a story in the *Daily Express* and *Daily Mirror* to give a modern illustration).
5. If time permits, investigate words of a carol. Do they come from the Bible account?

Year 6 [Age 10–11] – Life as a Journey

Travellers

1. Study in detail the story of the Three Wise Men (see Matthew chapter 2).

2. Get children to write "a Wise Man's Diary" (their traditional names were Caspar, Melchior, Balthasar), but give them a question for each stage of the journey

   (a) Do you really believe that stars give guidance?
   (b) Who or what were you expecting to find?
   (c) What did you feel about Herod?
   (d) Was your gift appropriate?

3. Discussion topics. These topics are about the children themselves, not in the Wise Man Role.

   (a) Who or what gives you guidance – are there good and bad influences?
   (b) What are you hoping to achieve in your life?
   (c) Who or what could help you/hinder you?
   (d) If you had taken a present to the baby Jesus, what would it be … and why?

Assessment, Recording and Reporting in RE

You can't assess RE. It's too personal.

That is a common response when we run courses on assessment in RE. We disagree. If RE is treated as an educational activity its outcomes should be as open to scrutiny as those of any other subject.

Reasons for Assessment

Consider this list produced by a group of final-year student teachers, although they don't claim to have said the last word on the subject!

- To find out what pupils know, understand and can do

- To help me decide where to begin in my teaching

- To enable me to give feedback to the children

- To help me to evaluate my teaching

- To inform me when I start to plan the next session

- To enable me to pitch activities more appropriately to children's abilities

- To provide evidence for writing reports

- To enable me to pass on information to the next teacher/school

- To provide material for me to record so that I have a sound basis of evidence to work with

- To give the children a chance to set targets for themselves and see how far they have been able to meet them

- To help me to work out why a child is having difficulties so that I can plan ways to help

It would be difficult to argue that any of these points is irrelevant to RE. Yet teachers often have a sense of unease about assessing in the subject, usually because of a feeling of trespassing into a child's insights and beliefs. The following extract from a school's RE policy reveals an approach which has been very carefully considered.

Extract from a School's RE Policy

ASSESSMENT, RECORDING AND REPORTING

Assessment incorporates observation of the processes involved, examination of the finished work and discussion with pupils. It is not the intention in RE to assess the pupils' beliefs or lack of them. It is, however, appropriate to judge the extent to which their understanding of religion is based upon accurate knowledge and developed skills. Assessment will also seek to identify their capacity for expressing opinions clearly and thoughtfully, for appreciating the opinions of others and for discussing differing points of view in a suitable manner.

Assessment takes place at the end of each topic. A record is kept of the work of each class on each topic. Notes will be kept of points of particular significance regarding the work of individuals, and important pieces of work will be considered for inclusion in children's assessment folders.

An overall comment on children's progress in RE will be included in the annual written report to parents.

This school has made a distinction between the two attainment targets. For AT1 ('Learning *about* religions'), it is clear that there is a body of knowledge that can readily be assessed: Jesus was born at Bethlehem, Jews worship in a synagogue, Muslims fast during Ramadan. Teachers can also consider children's understanding of such information. For AT2 ('Learning *from* religion') the issue is one not of assessing the beliefs and opinions that children hold, but of their ability to frame and articulate those insights and to consider thoughtfully the points of view of others. This is clearly assessable.

Is the workload manageable?

A pragmatic approach is taken by this school to the workload entailed in assessing RE – rightly so in our view. A strongly interactive approach to teaching RE, which we advocate, requires the teacher to 'be' with the class, participating fully in their learning experiences. This calls for an economical approach to paper-based assessment and for an attentive interest in the reactions and achievements of individual pupils during lessons; interactive teaching demands interactive assessment, not tick-sheet driven schedules. We propose the following documentation as adequate:

- **Written plans** for the work of the class showing long-term (annual scheme), medium-term (half-termly unit) and short-term (single lesson) intentions.

- Carefully drafted **learning outcomes** which 'cash-out' the relevant part of the programme of study, and demonstrate a balance between the two attainment targets (see, e.g., pages 7ff.).

- **Evaluation** after each unit including coverage of work, general assessment of the attainment of the class and notes of particular significance regarding individual pupils' progress.

- The **pupils' work**, marked promptly, with interactive feedback. For example, the teacher might pose a question for the child rather than making a closed comment.

- An **annual report to parents**, available to the next teacher, detailing the child's attainment in relation to the work covered. Appropriate comments can be drawn from the learning outcomes.

If you are fortunate, you will be working from a syllabus which provides much of the key information for you, as the examples below drawn from the Oldham Agreed Syllabus of 1996 show.

A teacher using this syllabus had taught a unit of work to her junior class about the parables of Jesus and was able to draw upon the learning outcomes (described under **'So that they could, for example'**) in her reports:

> *K_____ understands something of the importance of the parables of Jesus to Christians. He is able to explain some interpretations of the main parables and can relate them to his own experience.*

Learning about Religions			Learning from Religion	
Key Stage 2 [Ages 7–11]	**Key Stage 1 [Ages 5–7]**	**Core Objectives**	**Key Stage 1 [Ages 5–7]**	**Key Stage 2 [Ages 7–11]**
Children should	**Children should**	**EXPRESSION**	**Children should**	**Children should**
a. develop knowledge of holy books and other important religious literature.	a. encounter some of the stories and other writings which are important to faith communities and begin to explore their meaning	Children will explore: **Holy books, sacred writings, art, dance, music, drama, architecture and literature as means of expressing religious beliefs and feelings**	a. enjoy stories from different traditions, and realise that stories from religious traditions often deal with concerns and feelings similar to their own	a. talk about stories which focus on values, relationships or religious teachings and consider the relevance of this teaching for their own lives
So that they could, for example	**So that they could, for example**		**So that they could, for example**	**So that they could, for example**
a. name the special writings which are important to faith communities studied; and describe some of their essential features.	a. remember the outline of stories they have heard and suggest why these stories are valued by the religious communities to which they belong.		a. respond to the spiritual or religious aspects of stories in the light of their own experience and thoughts.	a. describe some of the religious stories which teach us to care for each other and relate then to their own experience.
b. explain some of the interpretations of symbols, stories and language given by believers.			b. draw on stimuli from the natural world in their creative work.	b. draw on material which has arisen during times of stillness and reflection in their creative work.

From the Oldham Agreed Syllabus (1996)

Reflective Approaches Used in This Book

The methods we use are all-important if we wish the children:

- to find their work meaningful, whatever their faith position;

- to be able to reflect on motives, feelings and possible outcomes of courses of action;

- to be open and prepared to share their insights in a safe and supportive environment.

The methods suggested below are amply borne out in the practical examples that follow on pages 16–63:

Always start from children's own experience, and from what they know or think they know. Even as experienced teachers we can easily make false assumptions about children's knowledge. Brainstorming at the beginning of a lesson clarifies the starting-point. For example, during the first lesson of a series on the life of Jesus with 9–10 year olds the children were asked to brainstorm the word 'Jew'. The first three answers were:

> The little drops of water on the grass early in the morning.
>
> My mum said it before our Johnny was born. He's due any day now.
>
> Jesus was a Jew.

Before I could respond the rest of the class chorused:

> No, he wasn't!

How important it was for me to know this before continuing that first lesson!

Questions, well thought out, are crucial. The most important questions in life usually have more than one answer. They are generally about meaning and purpose in life; they are about beliefs and values, and children need to be challenged to grapple with the issues. We need to ask thought-provoking questions in such a way as to encourage the hesitant child. For example, 'I wonder why …?' is a good way to begin:

> *I wonder why Jews have a mezuzah on their doorposts?*
>
> *I wonder how Muslims feel as they prostrate themselves in prayer?*

There may be factual answers to these questions; nevertheless, it is better that the children have to think of possible answers for themselves. Given a chance children constantly surprise us.

> *Did anything particularly surprise or interest you?*

This assumes a positive response, and more often than not creates a positive response from even the most reluctant child. Always give children the opportunity to ask questions. We don't have to know all the answers. There are ways of finding out: research using books, ask someone, use the Internet …

Take what the children say seriously and value it.
On one occasion when a class of 10–11 year olds was asked to sit quietly in a church and use their senses of sight, hearing and smell, one child jotted down:

> I can smell dead bodies.

Back in the classroom the children shared their experiences, and they considered what it was that could be smelt. Another child then asked:

> What does happen to you when you die?

The teacher batted the question back to the class by saying:

> *People have different ideas and beliefs. What do you think?*

Practically every child contributed to the ensuing discussion, and they listened attentively to each other.

Whenever possible give children a choice of activity.
Life is largely about making choices, so let's begin now. Providing a choice of activity removes the likelihood of a child saying they don't want to do something. For example, in the work on the Beautiful Names of God in Islam (pages 18–19), the children were able to choose which name to think and write about.

Ensure there's time for reflection and discussion whatever the main activity.
There is rarely time for every child to take part in a class discussion but sharing with a partner provides everyone with a chance to speak, and may well empower the more reticent child to share with the whole class.

Develop aspects of a topic that particularly interest the children.
Teachers plan with the children in mind, but there also need to be opportunities to follow up points that arise during the lesson. For example:

> *Why do Muslim parents want the first word a baby hears to be the word 'Allah'?*

Everyone in the class doesn't necessarily have to cover exactly the same work.
The children may be asked to research different aspects of the same topic, and then share their findings with the rest of the class. For example, when learning about diversity of belief and practice regarding children and young people being welcomed into the fellowship of the Church (page 52), one group researched Roman Catholic practice regarding baptism, one group Church of England practice, one group Baptist practice, and one group Salvation Army welcoming practice.

At all times we need to acknowledge the diversity of belief and practice within every religion.
It's important that we start by looking at the similarities, and only then explore the differences. It's not our task to state which view may be right, but rather to reflect on why people might believe or take part in some religious practice; to try to begin to enter into their feelings.

If there is to be time for reflection and discussion there has to be a sense of urgency about the practical activity.
For example, in the work on bark (pages 35–37), the children were given only 15 minutes to do the activity so that there would be time for discussion and sharing.

We need to provide occasions when children can develop their imagination, intuition, creativity, and a sense of awe and wonder.
This entails opportunities for experiencing either in reality or imaginatively: for example, an opportunity to examine in detail some small part of the world, such as a poppy seed head, a shell or feather; an opportunity to wonder at the complexity and the uniqueness of life around us; a chance to create music for work on Creation or to use colour and form to express feelings.

RE should be interesting and relevant, and often fun, it should grab the children's attention from the outset and promote a positive attitude. For example, the introductory work on Hindu gods (pages 19–20) caught the children's interest and produced positive attitudes. It was also fun!

Note

In the examples of units of work on pages 16–63, contrasting typefaces are used to distinguish the teacher's questions and responses from those of the children, as follows:

- **The teacher's questions, comments and responses are in bold type like this.**

- Children's answers, questions and comments (oral or in writing) appear in this script fount.

Possible Learning Outcomes

This work on descriptions of God (pages 16–21) is designed to help children to:

- know that religious believers use metaphoric language to enable them to think and speak about God (AT1);

- appreciate that a name or title may convey meanings at a deeper level than the literal (AT2);

- reflect on the metaphors/titles used by various faiths to describe God and on the words they think best describe God (AT1/2).

Religious language is full of metaphors. This is because of the difficulty people of all religions experience when trying to describe the indescribable – God. By using metaphors the characteristics of the transcendent can be described and reflected upon as the following work shows.

By way of introduction the children brainstormed 'a good mother', thinking of as many characteristics as possible within sixty seconds.

Each table group was then given a sheet of paper on which was written one of the following:

> **a good king**
>
> **a good shepherd**
>
> **a good creator**
>
> **a good shield**
>
> **a good father**
>
> **a good judge**

Each of the six groups was asked to brainstorm their phrase, writing all the characteristics they thought of on their sheet, before sharing what they had written with the rest of the class.

As the words were read out the teacher wrote them on the board and the rest of the class were encouraged to add additional qualities.

The words were:

king	judge	father
ruler	fair	caring
kind-hearted	deciding	understanding
good leader	honest	cross
generous	understanding	kind
funny	good leader	strict
clever	thoughtful	helpful
understanding	stern	curious
kind	strict	funny
helpful	in charge	strong
courageous	listens	interested
good listener	in control	polite
	responsible	encouraging
	patient	thankful
		thoughtful

shepherd	creator	shield
courageous	God	repels (the enemy)
caring	artist	protects
reliable	authors	looks after
protects	builders	saves
leads	thoughts	helpful
thoughtful	ideas	
brave	inspirations	
understands	imagination	
(what he's doing)	patience	
relies on his dog		

Until this stage the children assumed they were having an English lesson! The teacher then asked:

Who might have all these qualities?

It's impossible to have all of them!

You might feel jealous of someone with all the qualities you would like.

God might have all these qualities.

Which quality would you like to have?

To be helpful
To be patient
To be encouraging

(These, and other answers, could be taken further. The children could all choose a quality and reflect on how they might achieve it (AT2).)

The teacher then asked:

How would you feel about meeting a person with all these qualities?

You'd feel small.
Excited – Amazed – Nervous
Sad for them because others might be unkind about their perfectness.
You'd be polite because you'd look up to them.

The children looked again at some of the qualities – kind-hearted, understanding, patient, helpful – and reflected on how these qualities would make a difference to how we felt about a person.

Further questions could include:

Would you want to talk with such a person?
Would knowing their qualities make a difference to what you said to them?

These questions could lead to a discussion about prayer and how one might talk to God.

At this point the teacher asked:

Why, do you think, have all these names and many more been used to describe God?

Gradually the children began to be aware of the inadequacy of language to describe the indescribable, and how useful metaphors are, particularly if we have time to reflect on their meaning.

With some classes this work has been further developed by asking each group of children to look at their original list of words and to underline about three which they felt best described God. These words were then shared with the class and written on the board.

One class list included:

caring	clever	helps
kind	good planner	firm
loving	patient	brave
cool	defender	mighty
provider	father	strong
generous	family	courageous
fair	protects	spirit
likes children		feeling

Here the underlined words are those that occurred more than once.

Each group was then asked to choose three or four words from the list on the board which they felt best described what God is like for Christians, and to share their words and be prepared to give their reasons.

This work could be extended, especially in a church school, by asking:

How might these beliefs that Christians could have about God affect the way Christians live their lives?

Possible Follow-Up Work

From the original list of names, the children could identify the specifically male ones and list their female equivalents to consider the characteristics of these and note any interesting differences.

Younger children might make a display of the characteristics they would attribute to God, each pair contributing one characteristic/ quality. This could form the basis of class sharing and discussion.

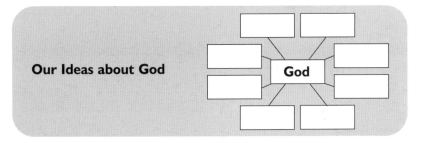

Our Ideas about God

God

First, the children discussed the meaning of their own names, and which name or nickname they preferred being called. There was also discussion about whether their names described what they were like.

This was followed by a sharing of positive qualities or characteristics:

Can you think of a quality that describes the positive side of yourself? We may not have that quality or characteristic all the time but we still feel it's an important part of ourselves.

Words such as:

cheerful, helpful, funny, reliable

were shared. Everyone was encouraged to suggest a positive quality.

The children were asked to draw a five-pointed star, to write their name in the centre, and a personal quality in each of the five points. They were encouraged to help each other if anyone became stuck. It was also suggested that each point be lightly coloured in such a way as to express the feelings associated with that quality.

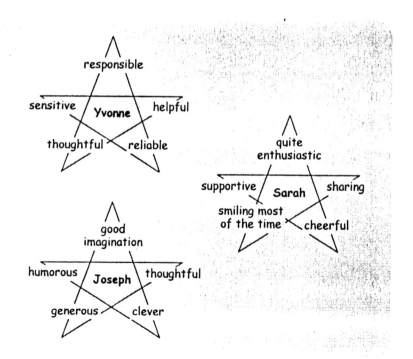

The teacher next checked that the children were familiar with the vocabulary she would be using in the lesson: 'Allah', 'Arabic', 'Muslim', and 'Islam'. She then said:

The Arabic name for God is Allah, but in order to describe what he is like Muslims use 99 descriptions or titles. Why do you think there are 99?

Ninety-nine's not quite a 100 per cent.

So what does that tell us?

That nobody can know everything about God.

Yes, only Allah himself knows all his names. Let's look at some of these 'beautiful names'.

The teacher wrote some of the names on the board:

The Merciful	**The Forgiving**
The Compassionate	**The Source of Peace**
The All-Knowing	**The Creator**
The Wise	**The Protecting Friend**
The Generous One	**The Guide**
The Loving	

Finally, the children were asked to choose one of the beautiful names of Allah; to write it out in large letters on A4 paper; to write the Arabic below, if they wished, and then to write down what they thought the name meant. (The Christian Education Movement booklet *Exploring Islam* proved very useful as it contains a number of the names in Arabic.)

Their ideas included:

<u>The Wise</u> – He knows everything. He tells people what is wise to do.

<u>The All-Knowing</u> – Someone who is always there when you need someone to talk to.

<u>The Guide</u> – He who leads you through life to bring out the best in you, and takes you on the right paths.

<u>The Forgiving</u> – God will forgive someone that has done something wrong.

<u>The Creator</u> – He made everything and also knows what is happening.

<u>The Merciful</u> – Allah or God is very merciful and takes pity on those who have done wrong.

The Many Faces of God in Hinduism

How can we introduce Hindu deities in such a way as to promote positive attitudes?

This can be difficult, particularly in those areas where children don't have the advantage of meeting Hindus on a regular basis. The following method, involving creating visual personifications, has been found to promote interest and respect.

The teacher first invited the children to help her create a figure to represent the Lord of Justice. He was given:

- three legs, so that he could stand firmly on the earth;

- five arms, one holding scales which are true, the other four warding off any interference;

- a single eye, for he must be single-minded;

- two large ears, so that he could hear well.

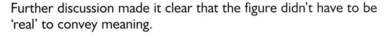

Further discussion made it clear that the figure didn't have to be 'real' to convey meaning.

Working in table groups, children were given a large sheet of paper per group and were asked to create a meaningful figure to represent the title written on the back of their paper. The titles were:

Lord of Time   **Problem Solver**
Message Giver   **Lady of Learning**
Lord of Power   **Lord of All Weather**

Having produced their co-operative efforts each group in turn invited the rest of the class to guess their title.

This was followed by discussion:

Does it matter whether the figures are 'real'/true to life or not?

Having created their own visual images the children were in a much better position to understand the visual images of Hinduism.

When the children were shown a picture of Ganesh, immediately they thought in terms of meaning:

Elephants never forget.
Elephants are very strong but can be gentle.

Though the answers weren't correct as far as the Hindu story of Ganesh was concerned, the teacher was satisfied that the children were looking for meaning behind the façade. She then told the story of how Ganesh came to have an elephant's head.

Further work could involve each table group finding out about one deity and sharing their findings with the rest of the class.

How Ganesh Came to Have an Elephant's Head

There are many versions of this story but here is one of the popular ones:

Parvati, consort of Shiva, was distressed because she had no son. Whilst Shiva was away Parvati decided to have a bath, but before bathing she rubbed oil all over her body and with the scurf from her skin she modelled a small human figure. Into it she breathed the breath of life, and named him Ganesh.

While she had a bath Ganesh guarded the house, and just at this time Shiva returned quite unaware that Ganesh existed. Similarly Ganesh had no idea who Shiva was so refused to let him enter the house. In a rage Shiva cut off Ganesh's head and forced his way into his own house.

Emerging from her bath Parvati saw the murdered Ganesh and was distraught. Shiva promised to restore Ganesh's life, and sent messengers out to every part of the earth to search and bring back the head of the first living creature that was found sleeping with its head facing north. A baby elephant was found lying in that position, its head was cut off, brought back and placed on Ganesh's headless body. He lived again, half man, half elephant.

What Do WE Think God is Like?

7–8 year olds

This approach could be used with any age group in the range 7–14 years.

If one asks children what God is like they usually describe him/her as being very old and having a long white beard. Such questions and answers don't promote reflection on the character or qualities of God. The following approach starts with the concrete but quickly moves to abstract thought and certainly does encourage reflection.

1. These 7–8 year old children began by playing the game:

If you were a _____ what would you be?

On a sheet of paper, each child wrote one answer for each of five objects named by the teacher, numbering their answers one to five.

The teacher warned the children that what they wrote down would be shared with their neighbour when the game had been completed. She encouraged them to write down the first answer that came into their head. No reflection was needed for this part! Here are two lists of answers, with the five words chosen by the teacher on the left:

1.	flower	snowdrop	rose
2.	vehicle	landrover	jeep
3.	colour	black	gold
4.	sound	horse neighing	laughing
5.	animal	pony	hamster

(Other objects one might choose are: a piece of furniture, an article of clothing or a tool.)

The children shared their answers with a neighbour and there was much mirth. Sometimes children were heard asking each other why they had chosen a certain object: the beginning of reflection.

The children were then asked to underline the word on their list that was most like them. As in circle time, every child was given the opportunity to share their word and give a reason for their choice, e.g.

pony, because he's soft and nice to ride
hamster, because he's cute and soft

When children discovered that they had, in some cases, chosen identical words it was clear that they were pleased. In such circumstances it's important that the teacher affirms those children who have chosen quite different words and are sometimes reticent at sharing them.

2. In the second exercise the teacher used the same five words, but this time the question was:

If God were a _____ what would God be?

The procedure was the same as described in 1, but in addition the children were asked to draw the word they had underlined and give the reason for their choice. (This would not be appropriate if there were Muslim children in the class.)

Here are some choices the children made:

God is like a dove because he likes peace.

If God were a flower he'd be a sunflower because he brings light to the world.

If God were a flower he'd be a rose near my grandma's grave.

God would be grass because there's lots of it, and God is over all the world.

God is like a whale, big and peaceful.

God is like a person because he's loving.

He's like a jeep. He can go anywhere.

Possible Follow-Up Work

As the children read their objects and state a characteristic or quality the teacher could write them on the board. The list would include words like:

> big and peaceful
> loving   strong   free

In pairs, or individually, children could choose three qualities they feel to be the most important when describing what God is like. These could be shared with the rest of the class and reasons given.

Sacred Writings: Rules and Laws

The Torah

6–8 year olds

Possible Learning Outcomes

This work on sacred writings (pages 22–28) is designed to help children to:

- know that religious writings contain moral guidance (AT1);

- know that they may contain rules about religious practice as well (AT1);

- reflect on rules that guide their personal behaviour (AT2).

See also additional possible learning outcomes on page 27 for work on the Torah and the New Testament.

Lesson 1

In an introductory lesson these children brought to school books that were special to them. They were asked to tell the rest of the class why their book was special:

> I like the pictures in my book.
>
> My gran gave me this book.
>
> I like books about dinosaurs.
>
> This is my reading book. It's special 'cos I'm reading it.

The teacher wanted to take them further in their thinking, so asked:

> **Do you read it on your own or with someone else?**
>
> **How often do you look at it or read it?**
>
> **Where do you keep it?**
>
> **How do you hold it?**
>
> **How do you feel if someone doesn't look after it properly?**

Lesson 2

In the second lesson the teacher showed the children posters and books with large pictures of the Torah. One was given to each table group and the children were asked to look at it very carefully so they could tell the rest of the class about it. The teacher encouraged them to think of questions they might want to ask. The only clue she gave them was that the pictures were about a very special book of the Jews called the Torah. As the children worked she went round from group to group.

After five minutes the children were brought together in a circle and as the pictures were shown to the whole class each group spoke about their picture. Whenever questions were asked the teacher usually directed them back to the class:

> **I wonder what the answer might be?**

All answers were valued. The questions asked in the first lesson were then asked about the Torah. The children learnt of its size, how it's dressed (and undressed), how it's carried round the synagogue, where it's placed so that it can be read to the congregation, where it's kept when it's not in use, how Jewish people might feel about it, etc.

The previous work on their own special book made the children more sensitive and understanding of the importance of the Torah to Jews.

Lesson 3

In the third lesson the teacher wanted the children to begin to understand what is written in the Torah. They looked at Hebrew script and then guessed what it said. 'Stories' was the only answer given. After agreeing that there were stories in the Torah, the teacher said that there were also rules to help people to live happily. Using several examples from Deuteronomy 22, verses 2, 4 and 6 (*Good News Bible*), she focussed on questions relating to the natural world. Rather than reading the verses, she asked the children (who had earlier compiled their own class rules):

> **What would be a good rule if you found someone's pet?**
> **What would be a good rule if you found a stray cow or sheep?**

All suggestions were accepted as of interest. The teacher then said,

> **Let's see what the Torah says,**

and read verses 1 and 2.

> That's what I said!

shouted one child excitedly. The same approach was used with verse 4, about donkeys, and verse 6, about birds.

The teacher felt it important that, even at this young age, the children should begin to learn something of the laws contained in the Torah, and she chose examples within their understanding, e.g. Deuteronomy 22:8, 24:19, 21.

Follow-up work could include children thinking of rules that would be appropriate to ensure the well-being of their pets, the well-being of people in their neighbourhood, etc.

Older children could examine rules affecting religious practice (see the following work).

The Mezuzah: One Aspect of Jewish Home Life

O rthodox Jewish homes usually have a mezuzah on every doorpost, except for the bathroom/toilet. The little boxes contain the Shema (Deuteronomy 6:4–9), the essence of Judaism, and one of the first passages learnt by heart by Jewish children. It is well worth spending some time and thought on the passage itself as it explains some Jewish practices, particularly concerning the home.

Questions worth exploring could include:

Why do you think Jewish people fix a mezuzah to most doorposts?

When entering a room, why do Jews touch the mezuzah and then kiss their fingers?

If children can't think of an answer ask them:

Why do you kiss? The answer may give you a clue.
Does it mean that Jews do it to show they love God? Can't you love God without doing that?

What do you think? (to class)
Yes, of course. (chorus)

Then why do you think Jewish people do it?

After a long silence one child ventured:

Perhaps it helps them to remember God.
Yes, I'm sure it does, and helps them to remember that God is always present and that their home is ruled by God.

How might they feel as they touch the mezuzah?

Follow-Up for Older Children

Having learnt what a mezuzah is, what it contains, and how and why it is used (AT1), a class of 9–10 year olds considered what was important in their own lives (AT2). They wrote down their ideas and put them in mezuzah-like containers which they had made.

Here are some examples:

> 1. Love and respect your parents always, and accept the punishments and privileges they give.
>
> 2. Do not buy ivory and mahogany ornaments because animals suffer on account of human greed.
>
> 3. Respect friendship and treasure it. It is a great thing and worth a lot, not in gold but in happiness.
>
> JENNIE

> Friendship is a gift that you should treasure as you would gold or silver.
>
> The meaning of life is to love, respect and treat others as you would yourself.
>
> Nature is a wonderful source of wisdom.
>
> Always be honest for honesty is better than any amount of cheating.
>
> Caroline.

This class had been learning about the Qur'an, how it should be handled, where it's kept, how it's used, etc., but most had little idea as to what it contained.

The children were asked:

What is the Qur'an?
It's the Muslims' special book.
The word of God.
The teaching of God.

Having accepted all these answers the teacher read a verse from the Qur'an:

To give generously in public is good, but to give to the poor in private is better. (Surah 2:271)

Are there any words you don't understand?
Yes, 'generously'.

The teacher directed the question back to the class and finally received the answer:

Give loads of stuff to people.

So what does the first part of the sentence mean?

As there were few answers she asked:

Why do some people give in public and not in private?
It's to make people think you're nice and kind.

There followed a discussion about motives.

Each pair of children was given a quotation, asked to discuss what it meant, and then to share their thoughts with the rest of the class. Here are the quotations and the children's responses:

It is most hateful in God's sight that you should say one thing and do another. (Surah 61:2–3)
God doesn't like us telling lies.
You say you'll be friends with someone but you're not.

Do not allow your hatred for other people to turn you away from being fair. Treat everyone fairly. (Surah 5:8)
Treat everybody the same.

Return evil with good, and he who is your enemy will become your dearest friend. (Surah 41:34)
You might be being bad but then decide to be good.
(They found this quotation difficult to understand.)

Be good to others as God has been good to you. (Surah 28:70)
God is kind to us. We are kind.
We give soup at harvest time to the homeless shelter.

God wants fairness, kindness and generosity to one's kindred. (Surah 16:90)
Treat everyone the same.
Generous means if you have a packet of crisps and give them all away.
If someone is hurt help them.
If someone is alone you could ask them to play with you.

You shall not kill one another. (Surah 4:30)
You mustn't kill one another.
If someone hurts someone in your family you shouldn't go and kill him.

Do not despise or laugh at other people, nor walk proudly on the earth: God does not love the proud and people who boast. (Surah 36:18)
Don't hate other people. Don't laugh at people. I think it's a good rule.

Whoever is sorry and mends his ways after doing something wrong shall be forgiven by God. (Surah 5:39)
If you do something wrong and sort it out God will forgive you.

There followed a discussion as to why this teaching was important.

In pairs the children then listed rules that they thought would be important to them, and from this list each child wrote down the one they considered the most important. If they wished they could surround it with an Islamic-type pattern, i.e. a pattern that is symmetrical and contains a mistake. The mistake indicates that even the best human effort is imperfect when compared with Allah.

Qur'anic and Biblical Teaching

The work on Qur'anic teaching could be done with 10 and 11 year olds and followed up by comparing quotations from the Qur'an with some from the Bible (see right and overleaf).

Each list could be discussed as to meaning and relevance to believers. Children could be asked to choose one saying and see whether they could find anything similar in the other religion.

The lists, copied onto different-coloured paper, could be cut up, and children, working in pairs, could see how many sayings could be matched.

The follow-up could include:

- the children sharing their findings;
- asking them whether anything surprised them, and why/why not;
- asking what are the similarities they've noticed between Christianity and Islam, and why there should be these similarities;
- asking what, then, are the differences (obviously, this question could be asked only if the children have already learnt about Muslim and Christian faith and practice);
- the children writing some of their own beliefs and stating why they think they're important.

Biblical Quotations

The protector of Israel never dozes or sleeps. (Psalms 121:4)

Lord, you have examined me and you know me. You know everything I do: You are all round me on every side; you protect me with your power. (Psalm 139:1–2, 5)

Thou shalt not kill. (Exodus 20:13)

[God says] You make unjust laws that oppress my people. That is how you prevent the poor from having their rights and from getting justice. That is how you take the property that belongs to widows and orphans. (Isaiah 10:1–2)

I will be with you always. (Matthew 28:20)

Biblical quotations (cont.)

Look at the birds: they do not sow seeds, gather a harvest and put it in barns; yet your Father in heaven takes care of them! (Matthew 6:26)

I tell you: love your enemies and pray for those who persecute you, so that you may become the children of your Father in heaven. (Matthew 5:44–45)

My commandment is this: love one another, just as I love you. (John 15:12)

… when you give something to a needy person, do not make a big show of it, as the hypocrites do in the houses of worship and on the streets. They do it so people will praise them. But when you help a needy person, do it in such a way that even your closest friend will not know about it. (Matthew 6:2–3)

Qur'anic Quotations

Return evil with good, and he who is your enemy will become your dearest friend. (Surah 41:34)

Be good to others as God has been good to you. (Surah 28:77)

Whoever repents and mends his ways after doing evil shall be pardoned by God. God is forgiving and merciful. (Surah 5:39)

You shall not kill one another. (Surah 4:30)

He knows everything on the land and in the sea; no leaf falls to the ground without His knowing it. (Surah 6:59)

He is with you wherever you are. (Surah 57:4)

There is no God but He, the Living, the Eternal. He neither slumbers nor sleeps. (Surah 2:255)

[God says] … you show no kindness to the orphan, nor do you vie [compete] with each other in feeding the poor. (Surah 89:12f)

To be charitable in public is good, but to give alms to the poor in private is better. (Surah 2:271)

Torah and New Testament

Possible Learning Outcomes

This work is designed to help children to:

- know that religious people, in this case Jews and Christians, have rules which affect their religious practice and personal behaviour (AT1);

- reflect on what they think is worth remembering in their own lives and how they would remind themselves of it (AT2);

- consider an important self-imposed rule in their own lives and how it affects their behaviour (AT2).

Lesson 1

The teacher brainstormed the following questions, noting on the board the children's ideas, and then used the lists to explore the answers further, especially those in response to the second question:

What are rules?
Why do we have them?

The teacher next asked:

What rules affect your lives?

At home
getting up, going to bed, being tidy, table manners

At school
not running in school, behaviour at mealtimes, behaviour in the playground
(The children considered which they felt most important.)

Outside school and home
Green Cross Code, Highway Code

Unwritten rules
courtesy and good manners

The teacher then told the children that they were going to explore some of the rules that are important to Jews and think why they might be important. She said that the first kind of rule affects what most Jews wear and their beliefs.

The teacher read Deuteronomy 6:4–9 and paused after each statement, asking such questions as:

What does it mean to say 'Love God with all your heart, soul and might'?

Why should Jews want to remember these words at all times?

Why should Jews be told to teach these to their children?

What kinds of reminder are used?

The teacher told the children that the second type of rule affects how Jews live their everyday lives. That is, it is about behaviour; what you do in certain situations. For instance, there's a rule about what you do if you find a lost cow or sheep. The teacher asked the children:

What do you think would be a good rule?
Now let's see what the Jewish rule is.

The teacher read Deuteronomy 22:1–4 and continued:

Do you think that's a good rule? Why/why not?

She then used the same approach with each of the following:

- a parapet round the edge of the roof (Deuteronomy 22:8);
- lending to the poor (Deuteronomy 24:10);
- using accurate weights so as not to cheat (Deuteronomy 25:13–15);
- punctual payment for a day's work (Deuteronomy 24:15);
- leaving part of the harvest for those in need (Deuteronomy 24:19, 21).

(Some of the Ten Commandments – Exodus 20 – could also be included.)

The teacher reminded the children that there were two types of rule and pointed out that some people were surprised that there are biblical rules about everyday living. She then asked:

Do you think it's important to have rules about everyday living? Why/why not?

Out of the discussion came the idea that what one believes affects how one behaves.

The teacher recalled that Jewish people have things to remind them of what is important in their lives – the mezuzot, the tefillin and the tallit. The children were asked to sit quite still for a minute and think of something that they wanted to remember at all times. Time was allowed for those who wished to share their thoughts, which the teacher wrote on the board. The children then wrote down what they wanted to remember and what would help them to remember, using ideas that were on the board or ideas that had not been shared.

Lesson 2

The teacher recalled that the children had looked at some Jewish rules and pointed out that Christians have rules too. Jesus obeyed the Jewish rules but he felt that two of them were the most important. The teacher read these rules (Mark 12:30–31) and asked:

Can you think of any reason why Jesus said they were so important?

(When discussing the second rule – to love one's neighbour as oneself – explain how this was part of Jewish teaching: see Leviticus 19:18. It is not a distinguishing feature of Christianity.)

Each pair of children was given one of the following passages from the Sermon on the Mount:

- Matthew 5:21–24;
- Matthew 5:33–37;
- Matthew 5:38–42;
- Matthew 5:43–48.

They were asked to read their passage and to be ready to share with the rest of the class what they thought it was about. During the sharing time, questions and further explanations were encouraged. The teacher added a question of her own:

What would happen if all Christians followed this teaching?

She then asked the children if they knew what she meant by a self-imposed rule. After discussion, she asked:

What rules would you want to follow in your life?

The children sat and thought about this for a moment or two. This was followed by a sharing time. The teacher then asked the children to write down their rule or law and what difference obeying this rule would make to their way of life.

This work could be followed up by making a display entitled 'Important rules in our lives and how they affect the way we live'.

Psalms and the Natural World

Possible Learning Outcomes

This work is designed to help children to:

- know something of one kind of biblical literature, i.e. poetry, particularly the structure and content of Psalm 148 (AT1);

- appreciate something of the complexity and variety found in the natural world (AT2);

- reflect on how this may affect religious people's understanding of God and their responsibility as believers (AT2).

The teacher explained how the psalms in the Bible were written as songs or hymns and that Psalm 148 is a hymn of praise. Discussion followed on the meaning of the word 'praise', including reference to dictionaries.

The teacher handed out copies of the psalm, read the first few lines and asked if the children noticed anything unusual.

Why do these lines all begin with 'Praise him'?
What do the words mean?
Why have I underlined certain lines?

She then pointed out the parallelism, i.e. that the second line in each pair reflects the meaning of the first. For example, 'heavens' could be called 'heights, and 'his angels' called 'his hosts'.

The teacher read the whole psalm and then the class read verses 1–4 and 13–14 with half the children reading each 'part', i.e. alternate lines. A class that enjoys choral speaking might like to read the whole psalm.

Following this the class brainstormed the things that people today might want to praise God for. These were written on the board.

The teacher then asked the children to choose some ideas for their own hymn of praise. Their first line could be 'Praise the Lord,' and if they wished they could end with that too. Some might like to use parallelism. Having discovered that there are 150 psalms in the Bible they decided to call theirs Psalm 151. Some examples are shown overleaf.

Psalm 148

	Verse	Parts for choral speaking
<u>Praise the Lord!</u>	1	All
Praise the Lord from the heavens,		1
Praise him in the heights!		2
Praise him, all his angels,	2	1
Praise him, all his host!		2
Praise him sun and moon,	3	1
Praise him all the shining stars!		2
Praise him you highest heavens	4	1
and you waters above the heavens!		2
<u>Let them praise the name of the Lord!</u>	5	All
<u>For he commanded, and they were created</u>	6	All
Praise the Lord from the earth,	7	1
you sea monsters and all deeps		
fire and hail, snow and frost,	8	2
stormy wind fulfilling his command!		
Mountains and all hills,	9	1
fruit trees and all cedars!		
Beasts and all cattle	10	2
creeping things and flying birds		
Kings of the earth and all peoples	11	1
princes and all rulers of the earth!		2
Young men and maidens together,	12	1
old men and children!		2
<u>Let them praise the name of the Lord,</u>	13	All
<u>for his name alone is exalted;</u>		All
his glory is above earth and heaven.		All
He has raised up a horn for his people,	14	Individual
praise for all his saints, for the people		
of Israel who are near to him.		
<u>PRAISE THE LORD!</u>		All

Psalm 151.

Praise the Lord!
Praise the Lord for my playful pets
Praise Him for Homely love
Praise the Lord for my loving parents
Praise Him for my friendly family
Praise the Lord for my sunny friends
Praise him for my relaxing peace
Praise the Lord!

Jo.

Praise the Lord!
Praise the Lord for my loving family.
Praise Him for my co-operative friends.
Praise the Lord for their wonderful love.
Praise Him for calm peace.
Praise the Lord for the darkness of the night.
Praise him for the bright light of the day,
PRAISE THE LORD!

Chloe

Creation: The Genesis Account

Possible Learning Outcomes

This work is designed to help children to:

- know the main outline of the creation story as told in Genesis 1:1–2:4 (AT1);

- appreciate that the story expresses the belief that God is responsible for the creation of the world (AT1);

- reflect on the responsibility of human beings for the world they live in (AT2).

The lesson began with a discussion about our knowledge of the world and how human knowledge is continually expanding.

The teacher then introduced the Genesis account:

> **We're now going to look at a very old story in the Bible, in the first book, called Genesis. Some people think it happened just as it's told, while others believe that it contains a message about God. One of things we're going to do today is to try and discover that message.**

The teacher then gave out typed copies of the biblical account (from the *Good News Bible*), one between two. Having children working in pairs ensured there was discussion. Each pair was asked to read about only one of the days of creation. Different verses were allotted to different pairs. They had to be ready to tell the rest of the class what they thought their verse meant and to ask any questions should they wish to. A sense of urgency was created by allowing only three or four minutes for this work to be completed. To make sure that everyone understood what was expected of them, the teacher read out the first two verses and a brief discussion took place followed by the children raising such questions as:

> Who made God?

> Is God true?

> The writer must have believed in God else he wouldn't have written it.

The children were asked:

> **Can anyone answer the first two questions?**

This led to a discussion on the word 'belief'.

The children set to work on their verses and then reported their findings and questions to the whole class. Some of the more interesting responses included:

> If there is such a thing as God, why doesn't everyone have a perfect life?

This provoked spontaneous replies which the teacher helped to unpack.

> It wouldn't be life if it were perfect, everyone would be the same.

> It would be good if everyone could do as they liked.

> If the world was perfect they wouldn't want to kill.

> I believe God sends challenges to see if you can get through them.

> Human beings are the bosses.

This comment (referring to Day 6) provoked much discussion.

> Creation is God's work. Human beings are his caretakers.

> The writer isn't a scientist.

> **How do we know? So what was the writer doing?**

> He was guessing. He was using his imagination.

General questions included:

> Who made the things before creation started?

> How big is God and why can't we see him?

> Why doesn't the power of God's words talk back when we pray?

Initially the teacher made no attempt to answer the questions, but redirected them, and the children attempted to answer them.

Next, the teacher encouraged the children to examine the whole passage and look for the following phrases/sentences (used in the *Good News Bible*):

> **Then God commanded …**
> **God was pleased with what he saw.**
> **Evening passed and morning came …**

The teacher then asked:

Why do you think these words are constantly repeated?

Why is there a seventh day?

In what way is this important to Jews and Christians?

What do you think is the main message of the whole story?

(That God is responsible for the creation of the world.)

Finally, the teacher offered the children a choice of written work:

- If you were creating a world what would you want in it? How would you feel if it was threatened with destruction?
- Write a poem or piece of prose entitled 'Caretaker of the World'.

Possible Follow-Up Work

- Express aspects of the story through movement (could be used with any class aged 7–14 years).
- Create sounds to represent each day of creation (could be used with any class aged 7–14 years).
- Use a limited number of colours and abstract shapes in art work to represent the whole of Creation.
- Write five commandments for the caring of the world.
- Write a five-line poem entitled 'Wonderful Aspects of Creation', with each line concerned with one of the five senses.
- Explore/research other creation stories.
- Draw two world shapes. On one write what makes the earth a good place to live in and on the other what spoils the world (could be used with any class aged 7–14 years).
- Consider what we can do to prevent the world being spoiled (could be used with any class aged 7–14 years).

> If people on my world were making destruction and war I would be ashamed of them and angry. I would be angry because they're not the kind of person I wanted them to be inside, and I would make them feel that way too.

> If I had the chance to make my own world I would have peace on my world and make sure that animals endangered would be protected and would live in peace also. I would have good education for children to get good jobs and to have a fair share in things. I would have kind human beings who will help and support people in times of need.

> In my world I would also have doctors and nurses to nurse the starving children abroad who have diseases (also people with diseases in our country).

Often children's writing is worth discussing by the whole class.

Appreciating the World in which We Live

This approach to the natural world helps children to really focus on one tiny aspect of it and to appreciate its importance. It is very much concerned with spiritual and moral development though it also has links with RE.

Poppy Seed Heads

Possible Learning Outcomes

This work is designed to help children to:

- be much more aware of one aspect of the natural world;

- begin to appreciate a believer's thoughts and feelings about creation and his or her personal responsibility for the ongoing creation of the world (AT1);

- to express their own appreciation for this part of the natural world (AT2).

First, the children examined a series of photographs of poppies in full bloom. They then shared their observations in as much detail as possible and the teacher wrote them on the board:

from black to purple in the centre
unusually big for a flower
bright red   orange red   pastel smudged
two together look like a tropical fish
a misty, purple planet with a red atmosphere
square black markings
a purple ball in a red cup
blood red with a black wound
a ball of fire with a black centre
a splodge of black on vibrant red
full with the breeze blowing
translucent   waxy   shiny
like a red spotlight

Semi-dried seed heads were distributed and again children examined them closely then shared their observations:

like an onion
like a pumpkin
a big air balloon
like a wine jug
big and bulbous as if it would burst

The teacher asked:

Why do you think the poppies have such large bright petals?

Notice how they're all similar and yet they're all different, all unique.

Notice how the shape of the seed head makes seed dispersal possible.

How was this design achieved?

The following visualization was then used (for guidelines on using visualization see M. K. Stone *Don't Just Do Something, Sit There*, pages 18 ff., RMEP):

We're now going to imagine what it might be like to be a seed head … Please sit in an alert and relaxed position with your hands relaxed in your lap and your eyes gently closed … Breathe slowly and deeply and be aware of your breath … In your imagination visualize/see the dried poppy head you were examining … Notice its shape, its colour, its size, its weight, the texture of its surfaces … Does it have a smell? … Now imagine you are that seed head … You've lost your petals … They have been blown away … Your stalk and seed head have dried and changed colour … Be aware of the dryness … Feel the gentle breeze rocking you as you stand among many other drying seed heads … Feel the seeds being shaken from you … Feel the warmth of the sun that has dried you and your seeds … You are left on a dying stalk – fragile and beautiful … How do you feel at this stage of your life as a poppy? … And now we're going to leave the poppies and return to the classroom … when you're ready, wriggle your toes, open your eyes and have a good stretch …

The teacher asked the children to share, in pairs, how they felt when they were a poppy seed head.

Which part of the visualization did you enjoy the most, the least?

Did anything surprise you?

The class were then asked:

Would anyone like to share how they felt when they were a seed head?

I felt heavy but happy knowing I was making more.
I felt reliable
motherly
helpful
like a mother with lots of children
proud
special
important
successful
strong
cheerful
fresh with the breeze

How did you feel when your seeds had gone?

sad and happy at the same time
as if my life had come to an end
when my seeds were gone I knew I'd never be the same
again
worthless
heart-heavy
fat
unhealthy
hot
doubtful
light
weak
alone
lonely
fragile
weary
deserted but free
sad because all the seeds in me had gone and started a
new life for themselves
upset to see them leave.
I can now lead my own life.

The children were encouraged to explain their thoughts and feelings.

Further discussion considered such questions as:

Why do you think there were positive feelings of being happy and negative feelings of being sad at the same time?

Is life like that? In what way?

Do you think all people experience happiness and sadness? Why do you think that? How do you deal with feelings of sadness?

The children were asked to describe their feelings as a seed head or seed in poetry, prose or words written on a seed-head shape.

I am a poppy seed high
  in the air
Burdenless explorer
Life adorer
What is there smaller
Than a poppy seed?

CAROLINE

Sickly full.
Seeds rumbling
  about inside
ready to burst out.
Overweight,
Miserable

BEN

As I get battered down
by the wind my seeds
get shaken out.
I'm on the ground now,
my work is done,
I've spread my seed,
Thank goodness,
Now I can rest.

STEPHANIE

Pretty
Scarlet red
Remembrance Day
Colour combinations
Vibrant.

STEPHEN

I felt proud that I was like the other plants.
I could feel the fresh air falling inside me helping
me to grow and my seeds as well. When the seeds
were blown out I still felt proud and I knew I would
never be the same again.

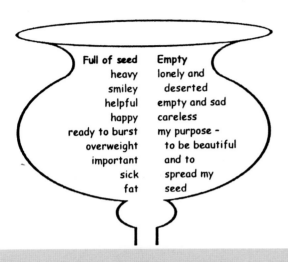

Full of seed
heavy
smiley
helpful
happy
ready to burst
overweight
important
sick
fat

Empty
lonely and
deserted
empty and sad
careless
my purpose -
to be beautiful
and to
spread my
seed

I am full and proud
Happy and still
I am a mother
Special, heavy.

Now I am empty
Lonely and old
Sad but happy
My end is near.   KYLIE

After the children had shared their work, the teacher likened the poppies to themselves. Poppies are unique as they are. There are differences and that's OK.

The poppy gave its seed to the world. What are gifts you have to give to the world?

The lesson ended with the children reflecting on this question and sharing their ideas.

This work could be extended by asking further questions:

Many religious people believe God is responsible for the creation of the world. If they looked at one part of creation in the same detail as you have, how do you think they might think and feel about God?

What responsibility have they for caring for the world?

Bark

Possible Learning Outcomes

This work is designed to help children to:

* be much more aware of one aspect of the natural world;

* know that people from ancient times, such as the writer of Psalm 148 or 104, believed that God should be praised for the wonders of the world (AT1);

* consider how we show our appreciation of the natural world (AT2).

Bark 1

The children were first asked to think of words that describe the bark of a tree. These were written on the board:

dull dirty dark cracked mucky brown

They were then given a piece of bark each and asked to explore it in detail: its shape, colour, size, texture, weight and smell.

They were asked to stick their bark onto a piece of A4 paper and to colour the paper in such a way as to camouflage the bark. They had a choice of medium – pastels, oil pastels, crayons or paint, together with charcoal rather than pencil. They were given only 15 minutes to complete as much as they could.

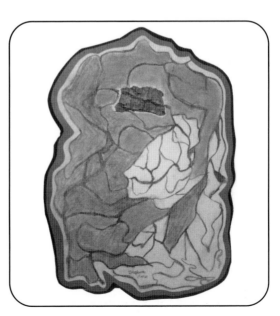

With their bark pictures in front of them they were asked to suggest further words to describe the bark. These words were also written on the board but in a separate list. They included:

speckled	amazing	many shades
swirly	wonderful	patterned
striped	fascinating	like a flowing river
colourful	full of life	

The children wrote poems making use of the two word lists on the board but were encouraged to think of additional words. Two types of poem were suggested and they were free to choose:

- to start their poem with 'I used to see bark as just bark …' and then to continue with 'But now I see bark as …';

- to write a poem containing the minimum of words – in this case nine – increasing then decreasing the length of line.

The children shared their drawings and poems.

Bark,
Unquestionably strange
Swirly, striped, squiggly
Knight's armour
Fascinating

TIM

I used to see bark as just bark,
dull, dusty and mucky.
But now I see bark as a pattern
of colours and full of life
like crazy paving, rough speckled
and a big shade of brown

SARAH

Possible Follow-Up Work

- Share practical ideas as to how the children are able to care for trees.

- The work described above isn't explicitly religious, but could be made so by linking it with Psalm 148:7–10 or Psalm 104:10–18. Discuss why religious people might want to write psalms at all.

- Brainstorm ideas as to why we might be thankful for trees. List them on the board. Ask children to write their own psalm of thankfulness for trees.

Bark 2: An Alternative Approach

The lesson began with the children examining their own piece of bark, and then discussing the function of the bark.

This was followed by a visualization (for guidelines on using visualization see M. K. Stone *Don't Just Do Something, Sit There*, pages 18ff., RMEP):

> Sit in an alert position … Gently close your eyes, and be aware of your own breathing; slow, deep and regular …

> Visualize/Picture in your imagination a tree covered with the kind of bark you've been examining … Think about its purpose to protect the tree from animals and insects, from stormy weather or excessive heat … to keep it warm and moist … Now imagine you are the bark on that tree, not just one bit of it, but covering the whole of the tree, the trunk and all its branches …

> You may be one tree among many or perhaps standing alone … What time of year is it? … Are you having to protect the tree from cold or heat? … Can you feel the moistness of the tree beneath you? … Feel its smooth surface … Be aware of the fragrance, the smell of the tree … You are protecting it from the weather, from animals, birds and insects … Each year you grow stronger and tougher, more able to do your job well … As the tree grows your skin may crack, but you are still able to fulfil your purpose … How do you feel about your life's work? …

> Now you're going to leave your tree and become yourself again and return to the classroom … Be aware of your chair and whether it feels hard or soft … when you're ready, open your eyes and have a good stretch …

The children were asked to share with their neighbour how they felt about the visualization, and whether anything surprised them. Class discussion followed around the questions:

> **What happens to trees if the bark is seriously damaged?**
> This brought out the realization that bark is essential to the life of a tree.

> **How did you feel about your life's work?**
> The answers for the most part were very positive, i.e. they saw themselves as having a vital role in life, though some saw it as extremely hard work, especially as the tree kept growing.

> **As human beings what can we do to help to protect trees?**

Like the work on poppies this work could end by reflecting on how religious people think about God and how this affects their behaviour towards the created world.

Trees

Sometimes very effective lessons may be based on very short passages from sacred texts.

These children spent time thinking about Jeremiah 17:7–8:

> **Blessed is the man who trusts in the Lord. He is like a tree planted by water, that sends out its roots by the stream, and does not fear when heat comes … it does not cease to bear fruit.**

> *Possible Learning Outcomes*
>
> This work is designed to help children to:
>
> * consider the needs of trees if they're to flourish;
> * understand why the metaphor of a tree is particularly apt in this quotation from Jeremiah (AT1);
> * reflect on what nourishes themselves (AT2).

The teacher introduced the lesson by asking questions about trees:

> **What does a tree need in order to live?**
>
> **What's the function of the roots?**
>
> **How do the roots affect the rest of the tree?**

Next, she gave out copies of the two verses, asked the children to read them quietly, then asked:

> **Why do you think the writer says that a person is like a tree?**

At the end of the discussion the teacher summed up what had been said:

> **The writer is saying that those who trust in God are like plants that have all they need, water and shade from the scorching sun, in order to grow well and produce good fruit.**

She continued:

In one way all people are like trees; they all need nourishment, things to help them grow.

What nourishment do we need as well as food and drink?

Following a class discussion the children were asked to sit quietly and think of something that was very important in their growth and development. A class tree was made and every child cut out a root on which they wrote whatever they needed as nourishment.

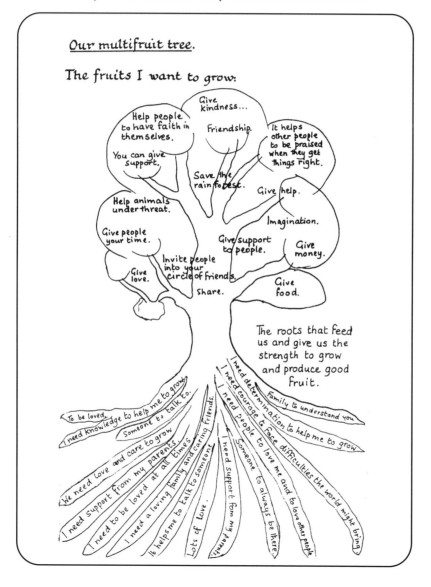

Possible Follow-Up Work

This work could be followed up with 10–11 year olds through visualization using pictures of trees (for guidelines on using visualization see M. K. Stone *Don't Just Do Something, Sit There*, pages 18 ff., RMEP):

Visualization 1

1. Choose a picture [of a tree]. Get to know it so well that you could describe it in detail to someone ... Decide on the time of day and the time of year ...
2. If you were in the picture where would you stand or sit? ...
3. Now imagine you are in the picture. How do you feel? ...
4. What can you see? ... hear? ... smell? ... Touch the tree nearest to you. Notice how it feels ...
5. What surprises or interests you most about the tree you touched? ...
6. If your tree could talk what question would you ask it? ...

Ask the children to share, in pairs, what they could see, hear, smell and touch. Then ask the class:

Which of your senses did you most enjoy using?
Is it a good thing that we have different feelings?

Share answers to questions 5 and 6, followed by general discussion.

What question would you ask the tree?
Do you like living in the rainforest?
What animals have lived in your tree?
Are you happy?
Tell me your history?
What's it like living in such a crowded place?
What sort of tree are you?
Why do your branches flop over?
Is it boring here all day?
Do you like being a tree?
What is it like with animals around you?

Visualization 2

1. Look again at your picture. Now imagine you are the tree near which you're standing/ sitting. Be aware of what you can see ... hear ... smell ... and how your roots feel as they seek nourishment from the soil ...
2. How long have you been growing there? ...

3. What have you enjoyed most about your life? …
4. What has been most difficult for you? …
5. If you could ask a human being a question what would you ask?
   …

Ask the children to write down their answers to questions 3 and 4 and follow this up with discussion.

Then ask them to write down the questions they wanted to ask a human being.

How would human beings answer these questions?

This could be followed up by asking:

Is there anything human beings can do to help these trees?

What have you enjoyed most about your life as a tree?

Children enjoyed sitting in my branches and I listened to them chat.

The sound of other trees and of animals.

Someone climbing in me.

I have enjoyed looking down on all the beauties of the rainforest and wondering what it would be like without this living green.

Giving out seeds and creating a forest around me.

Watching new baby monkeys learning to swim and scampering about.

Being a middle aged tree because it was really easy to handle.

Being big because when I was little I could have got stood on by a human. I've enjoyed looking at the high view from the top of the tree.

Listening to the birds sing.

Being able to see all the animals, trees and plants grow.

Getting above other trees because I love sunlight.

Having lots of animals in my branches when I have fruit.

Birds making nests in me.

The baby monkeys and jaguars playing, birds' eggs hatching and looking at all the colours.

Watching the waterfall because it looks and sounds beautiful.

What has been most difficult for you as a tree?

Being rooted to the spot.

Seeing all my family being chopped down.

Being scared of being eaten by a bird when I was a tree.

Getting at the sunlight because of other plants above me.

People cutting down trees because trees are important.

The threat of being cut down.

Watching other trees die because I knew it was horrible to die.

Growing up, because when I was young I might have been nibbled.

Getting above the very hard soil.

The wind blowing me about.

Just standing up and not walking.

Winter because my leaves have gone and I'm cold. All my animal friends were hibernating.

Being little because when you are big you have seeds.

As a tree, what question would you want to ask a human being?

What is the rest of the world like?

Are my ancestors still standing?

What's it like to be able to walk?

Does it feel good to move?

Why do you keep cutting us down?

Do you like being a human being?

What do you do all day?

What is life like as a human?

Is your life fun?

Why are some humans destroying us when they know they need us to live?

Possible Learning Outcomes

This work on places of worship (pages 40–51) is designed to help children to:

- know that religious people have special places where they congregate for worship (AT1);

- know about and appreciate the main activities which occur in a place of worship (AT1);

- realize that there is diversity within faiths (AT1);

- appreciate, through visits, how the place itself may help believers in their worship (AT1/2);

- reflect on their own special places (AT2);

- develop positive attitudes towards people and show a readiness to accept diversity of belief and practice (AT2).

When planning this work, one needs to be clear about the purpose of any visit to a place of worship. The focus is so often historical, architectural or even geological, and nor RE at all. It is also important that children visit several Christian places of worship during the primary years so that they learn something of the diversity in Christendom. Our task as teachers is to help children to begin to understand and appreciate diversity, first in Christianity and then in other world faiths.

If our visit is to a church, which is a place where community worship happens, and the focus is RE, then there must be elements of the work that focus on **worship**.

How can we help children begin to understand and appreciate what worship is and why people regularly worship together, when many children have little or no experience of corporate worship?

The examples of units of work in this section illustrate some approaches.

The following activity works better if children have practised the skill of being still, alert and relaxed. Strategies for teaching this skill are described on page 64.

On entering the place of worship the teacher asks the children:

Stilling in a church

Find a space away from other children and sit in an alert and relaxed position. Close your eyes gently and be aware of your own slow breathing. Now be aware of your senses and the messages they're giving you as you sit quite still.

What can you hear?

What can you smell?

Open your eyes. What can you see from where you're sitting?

Is there anything in this place that might help people in their worship?

Does this place provide any clues about what goes on here?

How do you know it's a (Christian) place of worship?

Make a note of anything that particularly interests or surprises you?

Study the notice board and any literature. What can you learn about this worshipping community?

Note down any question you wish to ask.

Not all these questions need to be asked during one visit, and the questions may be adapted or completely changed, but they should encourage and provide an opportunity for children to experience something of what it might be like for a worshipper, and challenge children's thinking.

Visit to a United Reformed Church

Here a worksheet provided questions different to the set on page 40 but along the same lines. The answers indicate the range of thinking and understanding of 9 and 10 year olds. The final section, in which children pose their own questions, was dealt with by the minister of the church.

1. How does it feel to sit here?

OK	peaceful
full of heaven	safe
happy	pleasant
nervous	bored
majestic	exciting

It feels like God is sitting next to you.

Comfortable and relaxing, but that might be because I come to this church on Sunday.

2. What makes me feel comfortable or uncomfortable?

nothing	the seats
comfy seats	it's warm and welcoming
having time to think	a place to be thoughtful
coldness	the foot rest and padded seats
loneliness	the echoes when you talk

The flowers make you feel at home.

It makes me think of my great granddad.

3. What might help people to worship here?

the quietness	it's warm and inviting
God	it feels safe
real silence	stories from the Bible
forgiveness	the vicar saying prayers

There might be some friends and probably songs and encouragement from the vicar (minister).

People who have been before telling others of the good things that happen.

4. Would it feel different if there were people worshipping here? How?

Yes, I wouldn't feel nervous.
Yes, I would be embarrassed.
No, because you're worshipping God as well.
No, because it will be the same.
No, I just like sitting here.
Yes, I would feel uncomfortable because I don't believe in God.

Yes, if they were making a lot of noise I would feel relaxed.

5. What does this worshipping community do? (See the notice board.)

Barnados, Christian Aid
They help people in need all over the world.
They help not just one day, but everyday.
They have a Sunday school.
They welcome people into the church.
They have tea for the older people who raise money for charities.

6. What questions do you want to ask?

(The minister answered these questions.)

Why do you think God is so important to people?
What do the letters on the cloth mean?
How old is the church?
Do you have a youth club?
Does the church have meetings?
Do a lot of people come to church?
What do people like about the church?
When you pray what do you say or ask?
Have you ever cried over people's death?
Are you nervous taking services?

A follow-up discussion is essential if misunderstandings are to be unravelled and children's thinking extended. In order to capitalize on children's experience, carefully selected answers given by the children should form the basis of the discussion.

- Here the teacher could point out that a variety of answers to questions 1 and 2 would be expected as everybody's different, and that it's perfectly acceptable to be different. Then the teacher can go on to wonder aloud why some children felt thoroughly at ease in the church and others may have felt bored.

- For the answers to question 3, the teacher might ask: 'What makes this place "feel safe"? What do you mean by "real silence"?'

- The answers to question 4 show the teacher that in spite of careful preparation some children thought they were there to

worship, whilst others clearly saw the difference between worship and an educational visit. As teachers it's important that we're aware of such misunderstandings!

- Discussion of answers to question 5 would make clear that this community wasn't concerned only with the internal organization of their own church affairs – Sunday school, tea for older people, making worshippers feel welcomed – but were also outward looking. They saw part of their witness as serving those in need.

- Question 6 produces profound questions, e.g. 'Why do you think God is so important to people?' This may not be about the place of worship but it's at the heart of religion. Encourage the class to help answer questions like this.

These children had already visited an Anglican church and a United Reformed church.

They were asked to sit quietly and see what thoughts came to them, to be aware of the message of their senses, and to consider how the people who worshipped there might feel.

After ten minutes of complete silence the children were brought together and asked if they had noticed any similarities with the other two places of worship. Apart from 'a Bible' the answer was 'no.'

The teacher then asked:

What have you noticed that's different from the other churches?
There's no pulpit.

What does that make you think?
P'raps they don't have any notices.

They do have notices, but pulpits in churches are used for something else too. Does anyone know?
For the vicar to talk to you.

Right. I wonder why Quakers don't have pulpits?
Doesn't anyone talk to them?

People do talk, yet they don't have a pulpit. I wonder why that is?
Perhaps a lot of people talk, so one pulpit wouldn't be enough.
The benches are in a square facing each other.

What does that make you think?
Nobody's more important than anyone else.

You're right and anyone present may feel God wants them to speak, or pray, or read from the Bible or another book.
There's no organ or piano.
And no hymn books.

What does that make you think?
They don't sing.

No, they don't usually sing in a Meeting for Worship.
There are some books on this table (which was in the centre).

Why do you think the table is there?

After following this up:

What are the other books?

This provided a chance to talk briefly about *Advices and Queries*, which is read regularly in Meeting for Worship, and *Quaker Faith and Practice*.

Questions the children asked included:

How does the meeting start?

Why are there flowers on the table?

Do they have a vicar?

Does anyone get bored?

Do they baptize children?

Do people get married here?

In every case the teacher encouraged the other children to try and answer the questions. Before leaving the meeting house the children were told that the full name for the Quakers is the Religious Society of Friends.

After the visit the children expressed their feelings through art, movement, music and poetry.

The Friends
To the left hand side of my picture is the opposite of what I felt like in the meeting house. There is a picture of a gravestone you might usually find. It looks spooky. There is also a square spiral. It is wound up.
There is a light blue line for a fresh beginning when I walked through the door.
The square spiral unwinds into a soft green line. The snowdrops are a sign of life. Eventually the line comes back on itself, and there is a gravestone in the middle. It doesn't look spooky at all.
The colours are calm and there is a protecting brown line round it. The dove is a sign of peace.'
Joseph

Visits to Different Christian Places of Worship

Though the topic had been chosen by the teacher and introduced by visiting places of worship, the follow-up was determined by the children for much of the work focussed on:

• what interested the children,

• the questions they asked.

These children visited three churches and on each occasion were asked to sit in a pew some way away from any other children and to look quietly around and to note down anything that interested them.

After a short while they were asked to sit relaxed but alert with their eyes gently closed and to be aware of their feelings and any thoughts that came to them.

The children were then asked what might help people to worship there.

Finally, they were asked to jot down any questions they wanted to ask.

Back in the classroom the children examined posters and wrote down their questions. These were used as a basis for discussion. The children were encouraged to work in pairs. This stimulated discussion.

The Friends Meeting House (Quakers)

What's the most interesting thing you can see?
The balcony but there are no stained glass windows. Everything is wood, everything is very plain. All the wood is old.
The balcony looks very old but beautiful.

The seating arrangement.
The pictures are interesting.
The room smells of wood. It's a lovely smell.

What were your feelings and thoughts as you sat in the quietness?

Safe Still
Calm and happy
It's very peaceful.
I imagined what it was like 300 years ago.
Peace like a dove.
I thought about my friends and the people in the third world.
I thought it would be like a church but it isn't. It's quiet and peaceful, warm and comfortable.

What might help people to worship here?

It's quiet.
You can think your thoughts.
Because it's silent.
There is nothing to distract them.
Because some people might like to sit silent.
It has a nice atmosphere. I feel really welcome.
It's quiet, warm and comfy.

What questions would you like to ask?

Was the balcony built with the meeting house?
Why are the benches facing different ways?
Why do you have cushioned benches?
Can people get married in their meeting house?
Why isn't there a cross in the building?
Do the pictures on the wall signify anything?
Why are the stairs wonky, or have they worn out over the years?

The Anglican Church

What's the most interesting thing you can see?

The stained glass windows, because they tell stories.
The bird stand (lectern).
The eagle because of its shape.
The hawk bookstand.
The memory stones (memorials).
The hole in the wall. Did a statue fall from it?

The small room inside the church (Lady Chapel).
The shields on the roof.
The patterns in the wood.

What were your feelings and thoughts as you sat in the quietness?

Peaceful warm happy relaxing lonely
My granddad's funeral.
I thought about my gran who is dead.
I thought about some of my relations who have died.
I feel warm and safe when sitting inside this church.
The gold cross makes me feel warm.
Weird. What I was going to do when I got home tonight.
I felt like I was praying.
It feels very quiet sitting in silence on my own.
A lovely quiet peaceful place.

What might help people to worship here?

It's a calm and quiet place and has things to remind you of God.
The stained glass windows give people ideas to think about.
It's big and not colourful and exciting so you won't be bothered to open your eyes.
By looking at the cross at the front.
To help them forget about people that they had lost.
The quietness and stillness and the crosses around the church.
It is silent, and people can come here to pray to God if they have done something wrong.
It's quiet and you can solve problems.
It's got a pleasing, warm, caring silence.

What questions would you like to ask?

What is the bird for (on the lectern)?
Why is it an eagle?
What does 'MU' stand for?
Why is there a roof on top of the pulpit?
Is the vicar meant to be like Jesus?
Where are you baptized?
Why are there gravestones on the floor?
Why does the Lady Chapel have blue kneelers?
Why is there a picture in the Lady Chapel and nowhere else?

The Essentials of a Christian Place of Worship

These children had visited three local Christian places of worship: Anglican, Methodist and Quaker. In a class discussion they were asked:

What do you think are the essentials of any Christian place of worship?

Their ideas included:

All the people to believe in God.
All have places of worship and seats.
All have people.
They all pray.
They all have Bibles in them.
They all have Sunday schools if there are young children.

Then each table group was asked to write down what they considered to be essential. The quality of the discussion is reflected in this group's ideas:

1. A Bible.
2. The right atmosphere.
3. People who are willing to worship.
4. People who care for the place of worship and are responsible for it.
5. Somewhere big enough.
6. Meetings to discuss important matters concerning the place of worship.
7. A God.
8. Everyone belonging to that religion to be satisfied.

In the final exercise each table group was asked to record their personal feelings about religion:

Our thoughts on Religion (Group 3)

Peter thinks that there should be lots of different religions and churches because everybody's different.

Elizabeth M thinks that people should have the freedom to worship what they want.

I think that there shouldn't be religion because it only causes wars and trouble. I think if there has to be a religion it should be like a big family. As well as this, it would help to stop nations fighting and to help all the world's countries to come together and be friends.

Elizabeth F agrees with Peter and Libby, but she thinks the Quakers have a strange and much different way of doing things to other Christians.

These children were preparing for a visit to a mosque but the approach could be used for a visit to any place of worship.

By way of introduction the children were asked to work in pairs addressing questions that were written on the board:

> **Have you a special place?**
> **Where is it?**
> **What makes it special?**
> **What do you keep there?**
> **When do you like to go there?**
> **Do you invite anyone? Who? Why?**
> **How do you feel if someone doesn't behave respectfully?**

The class discussion that followed highlighted many similarities in their ideas.

Working in pairs or alone, the children were asked to write their answers to the question:

> **What advice would you give to someone visiting your special place?**

Kerry wrote:

> First tell me you're here, don't just walk in. Be sensible. Handle special things with care. Only get giddy and silly if we're having a laugh. Don't look in my diary! Don't take down my pot dolls. Don't mess with old and special things.

Photographs of the inside of a mosque were shown and the children were told how Muslims would conduct themselves before and during worship. Again, working in pairs or individually, the children were asked to answer the question:

> **What advice would you give to someone visiting a mosque?**

Chris wrote:

> Be respectful. Take your shoes off before going in. Cover your head. Wash before using anything. Be quiet in the prayer hall. Ask permission before using anything. Be polite. Don't eat or drink inside.

Sharing what had been written led to a discussion of what is appropriate for a visitor who wishes to show respect but not necessarily belief.

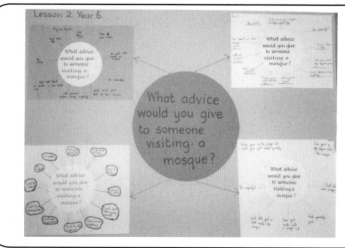

Books in Churches

A visit to a church might have a very limited focus, such as books. The work could be through children's research and based on the following questions:

- Write down the title of a book used in this church.
- Look inside. What is the book about?
- Who uses the book?
- Are there any clues telling you how and when the book is used?

- Is there a large special book? What is it called?
- Where is it placed? Why?
- Does this tell you anything about the beliefs of the worshippers?
- Is it open or closed? Why is this?

- Is there any other writing in the church?
- Choose one piece of writing. What information does it give you?
- Does it tell you anything about the church or the people who worship there?

Books in
Churches

_____

7–11 year olds

The Torah in the Synagogue

A visit to a synagogue might also have a limited focus, e.g. the Torah. The questions we ask need to give meaning to the Torah. Facts alone are insufficient. Children need to be encouraged to be reflective and to consider the possible feelings of the worshippers. For example:

- Where are the Torah scrolls kept?
- Can you think why?
- Why are they 'dressed up' and decorated?

- Why is the scroll which is read during the service lifted up high and carried around the synagogue?
- Why do you think people touch it with their prayer shawl or prayer book?
- What does this tell us about Jewish belief?
- When you were shown a scroll how was it handled? Why?
- Why is there more than one scroll in the Ark?
- Why do you think the Ark is at the front of the synagogue?
- Why is the Torah so important to Jewish people?
- Why should anyone obey laws and not just do whatever they want?

The Torah
in the
Synagogue

_____

7–11 year olds

Follow-Up to a Synagogue Visit

The teacher asked each child to make a plan of the synagogue from memory and name any parts. From this initial activity there was class discussion – starting with the furniture and objects and then moving on to 'Who?', 'How?', 'Why?', 'When?' questions. The children were also encouraged to ask their own questions. Their questions and comments included:

Why are there no statues or pictures of people in the synagogue?

It's dangerous to have pictures of people in the synagogue. People might worship them instead of God.

How did they get the scrolls from the Ark to the bimah?

Why did the women sit on the ground floor and not in the balcony?

What did they sing?

Why don't they use a book instead of a scroll?

In groups the children were asked to list several similarities to Christian places of worship (which they had visited the previous term) and several features that were different.

Follow-Up to
a Synagogue
Visit

_____

10–11 year olds

Similarities		Differences
Candles	Service book	Torah scrolls
Balcony	Children's class	Kippah
Memorial plaques	Sing	Tallit
10 Commandments	Worship	Hebrew writing
A place to read the scriptures		

They were asked why they thought there were so many similarities, and the common heritage of Christians and Jews emerged.

Each group researched one aspect of Judaism from books, posters and artefacts and then presented their findings to the rest of the class. The topics were the synagogue, the Torah, the Sabbath, Hanukah and artefacts. The presentations included making objects and talking about them, and an opportunity for the class to ask questions:

Synagogue
How long is a service?
How many different services are there in a week?
Do all synagogues face in the same direction?
Why don't men go into the gallery?
Why do they have an everlasting light?
Do they light candles in a service?
Do they sing in Hebrew?

Making a Torah scroll and mantle

Torah
Why do they have so many scrolls?
How much do they cost?
Is the Torah as long as the [Christian] Bible?
How long does it take to read the Torah?
Do Jews call God by a different name?

Sabbath
Do they have a special meal every Sabbath?

Hanukah
Why do some candlesticks have seven candles and some nine?
When do they light them?

Artefacts
Do Jewish people always wear a kippah and a prayer shawl?
Does a rabbi have a special costume or uniform for different occasions?
Why do they have kippahs and prayer shawls?
Why do the men wear kippahs and not the women?

General questions
Are Jews allowed to support a football team?
Do rabbis wear dog collars?
Can they have pets?
Do they go to the pub?

(Such questions provide a marvellous opportunity to challenge stereotypes.)

Having made a kippah one child tried to imagine how he would react if he were seen wearing one:

I was walking down to the synagogue and I had my kippah on. A group of boys stared at me and jeered. I tried to ignore them and just kept on walking but they followed me. They yelled rude things at me and started throwing pebbles. I started walking more quickly. They shouted, 'Scared are we? Running away with your precious pretty hat. I don't think it will keep you warm.' I was nearly there. I ran the rest of the way. I was in the synagogue, safe at last.

Planning Visits to Places of Worship

Make sure the visit is planned in accordance with LEA guidance on Health and Safety. Make a preparatory visit. Clarify the purpose of the visit with the priest, minister, rabbi, ... It is educational and not an opportunity for evangelism. (Children should not be asked to take part in any act of worship.) This is a time to collect information about the place of worship but also to discover any particular requirements, e.g. covering heads. Confirm the agreed date and time in writing. It's often worth making a phone call immediately prior to the visit to be sure there isn't a funeral at that time.

Notify **parents** in advance of the proposed visit. Make clear its purpose and how it contributes to the RE scheme of work. Explain that the children will be there to listen, observe and learn, and not to participate in any act of worship. Invite parents to accompany you. Such parents become your best ambassadors. If any parent is uncertain about the visit try to arrange to speak with them and reassure them.

Consider what attitudes you want the children to develop and how you're going to give the necessary opportunities for such development to take place, e.g. respect would be shown in the children's behaviour. You can make it a positive experience by asking such questions as:

What interests you?
What puzzles you?
What questions do you want to ask?
What have you learnt?
What have you noticed?

These questions are open ended to allow children to explore their own ideas and interests and to encourage them to frame questions that spring from a respectful curiosity,

How and where are children's questions to be dealt with? Is a religious leader or lay person able to answer questions during the visit?

The children's responses will help the teacher to gauge the existing level of their understanding and to identify any who may be apprehensive, or possibly prejudiced.

Have clear learning objectives. What do you hope to get out of the visit? Do the children know as well? In a possible question/answer session at the end of the visit the teacher should be prepared to supplement questions or answers if this is felt necessary. You are in charge. With older children you want to get beyond 'What do the Christians/Muslims/Jews/... do?' to 'What does it/they tell you about what these Christians/Muslims/Jews/... believe?'

Types of activity you could use include:

- Observing – symbols, colours, objects. Where are they situated, and why? What is everything for? Who uses them? What books are used? Why? When? What posters and notices are there? What do they tell us about this worshipping community? Make it a problem-solving activity.
- Listening to music, a speaker, each other.
- Asking questions.
- Sitting in silence to appreciate the atmosphere, the splendour/simplicity of the building; using the senses – seeing, hearing, smell, touch.
- Taking photographs – if permission has been granted.
- Drawing some object that interests the children. Putting in objects on a plan of the building.

Note Not everything that is used in the building will be out on display, e.g. a chalice or baptismal register. If the priest/minister is present in a church, for example, he/she might be asked to wear his/her vestments, or simulate a baptism.

After the Visit

Send a letter of thanks from yourself, or better still, from some of the children highlighting different aspects that particularly interested them.

Possible Follow-Up Work

- Researching using books and posters. Compare what is found with what the children have experienced. Make use of any photos taken. Why, for example, are 'churches' different – even those belonging to the same denomination? What are the essentials in a place of worship?
- Drawing and painting aspects that particularly interest the children.
- Clay modelling of objects, e.g. a lectern, font, pulpit, chalice. Add a caption explaining its significance.
- Writing – creatively/poetically about one's feelings; descriptively about one object, e.g. a stained glass window; a letter to a friend about those aspects you found interesting; an illustrated guide showing the building's importance to the worshipping community.
- Creating a display or make a book about that place of worship.

Note During their primary years children should have the opportunity of visiting several places of worship. They should not be encouraged to compare them in terms of 'This church is better than that', but rather, 'How might this place of worship help the people who worship here?'

Introduction to Special Places

Suitable mainly for use before a visit but worth looking at again afterwards to note the similarities between one's own special places and a sacred place.

My Special Place

| What I have in my special place | Draw a picture of your special place | What I do in my special place |

Who I invite and why

How I feel in my special place

For a Visit with 7–9 Year Olds

Alternative front pages
- The name of the place
- Welcome to …
- A sketch of the building
- The doors sketched on

Alternative questions for 9–10 year olds
- What was the first thing you noticed when you entered the building?
- Sit somewhere quietly on your own. How do you feel?
- Which picture/statue/symbol attracts your attention? Why?
- What do you think attracts people to this place of worship?
- What clues are there which show what happens during worship?
- Has anything surprised you about this visit? Explain why.
- What do you want to remember most about this visit? Give your reasons.

Such questions are appropriate for use in any place of worship, e.g. in a synagogue or mosque, not just a church, though the questions could be more religion specific.

For a Synagogue Visit

Are there any clues on the outside of the building that tell you this is a synagogue?

In addition to focussing on the artefacts and furnishings, the children should be encouraged to consider the synagogue as a place of worship; to sit and absorb the atmosphere and reflect on what might help people to worship there.

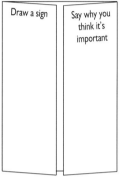

Diversity in Christian Initiation

10–11 year olds

Possible Learning Outcomes

This work on special/sacred times (pages 52–53) is designed to help children to:

- know something of the diversity of belief and practice in Christian initiation (AT1);
- reflect on the differences in Christian initiation (AT1);
- know something of Jewish and Islamic initiation (AT1);
- reflect on possible reasons for these practices (AT2);
- reflect on the kind of ceremony they would want for their children (AT2).

The teacher began by asking the children how they came to have their forenames, thus ensuring that all children felt included. She then told the class that for most Christians baptism was a time not only for naming a child (christening) but accepting them into the family of the Church.

Some of the children had been baptized, and they shared with the class what their parents had told them. Some brought christening presents to school. Others spoke of being present at the baptism of a relative.

The children were split into four groups and were told that their task was to find out all they could from the books and posters provided. They should also list any questions they wanted to ask. Each group researched one denomination's practice:

- Roman Catholic
- Church of England
- Baptist
- Salvation Army

Each group reported what they had discovered and the rest of the class had an opportunity to ask questions.

The class as a whole were surprised to learn of even some of the variety of belief and practice in Britain. Many children didn't know of the believers' baptism as practised by Baptists, or that the Salvation Army didn't baptize children but rather had a service of dedication and thanksgiving.

There was a choice of written work; either something about their own or someone else's baptism, or about the practice of a particular denomination which they had researched.

My Christening

When I was christened I had a triple christening with my cousins. Andrew is the oldest. He had to wait 7 months before Elaine and I were old enough. We had a triple christening because our family wanted a big party afterwards. We were christened at St Andrew's Church.

RIA

An account of a recent baptism

Mrs S. had invited us to her grand-daughter's christening. It was a private baptism at the back of the church. The Godparents and parents stood round the font and made all the promises they have to make. The baby didn't cry. The service commenced and after hours of photography, we left for Mrs S's huge house. When we arrived there was a massive table of food and a cake. Dad said grace and we all dived in. Everyone had a great time.

DAVID

This kind of writing calls for further discussion:

What are godparents for?

What promises do they make?

Why do many Christians think it's important for young children to be part of the church family?

Jewish Initiation

Having learnt something about Christian initiation these children next researched Jewish practices. They were asked to note down anything that surprised or particularly interested them, and to be ready to share this with the rest of the class. Here are some examples:

Some people plant trees to celebrate a birth; cedar for a boy and a pine for a girl.
I wonder why? (asked the teacher)

Names are very important. Many come from the Jewish Bible: Sarah, Rachel, Ruth, Deborah, Esther, Rebecca, Leah, Isaac, Jacob, Daniel, Simon, Samuel, David, ...
If your mother is Jewish then you're Jewish.

Some Jewish communities say that if you're brought up as a Jew and your mother isn't a Jew you can still be regarded as being Jewish.

(A good example of diversity within Judaism.)

The ceremony – Brit Milah (circumcision) – takes place on the eighth day of a baby's life. It is then that the baby is given a name.

A girl's name is usually announced in the synagogue on the Sabbath after her birth.

Muslim Initiation

Having learnt something about Christian and Jewish initiation the children were asked to research Islamic customs, and to note down points of interest. Here are some:

The father usually decides what the baby's name will be. Straight after being born the baby has a bath. Then, usually it's the father, who whispers a special prayer in the baby's ear.

Why?

Perhaps it will help the baby to understand who Allah is if they hear prayers lots of times.

I think they want the baby to believe in God.

When the baby is young all the hair is shaved off. It shows that the baby is having a new start. Many Muslims weigh the hair and however heavy it is they give that amount of silver to charity.

In Muslim countries goats or sheep are sacrificed for a feast. Why do boys get two goats and girls only get one?

When a baby is born they put sugar or honey on the baby's tongue. Does it make the baby sweet and friendly?

They say a lot of prayers. Why?

Other questions included:

What does 'Allah' mean?

Why do they use this name?

Why do parents want the first word they hear to be the word 'Allah'?

Why do Muslims keep repeating words when they say their prayers?

Why does the father speak to the baby when it can't understand what he is saying?

After each question the teacher encouraged other children to attempt to answer.

Possible Follow-Up Work

Ask each child to consider:

If you were a parent what kind of ceremony would you want for your child?

Possible Learning Outcomes

This work on Pentecost (pages 54–58) is designed to help children to:

- be able to relate the biblical account of Pentecost and what happened as a result (AT1);

- understand the use of symbolism and the power of the images of wind and fire (AT1/2);

- be able to express the biblical account in a non-literal manner and to share their thoughts and feelings with other children in the class (AT1/2);

- reflect on personal experiences of feeling empowered (AT2).

Note For examples of work on the Resurrection, see the companion book Ewens, A. & Stone, M. K. *Teaching About Jesus* (RMEP).

The Christian festival of Pentecost is omitted by many schools, but this church school felt it important. The class began by examining the words 'fire' and 'wind', which are so important in the biblical account (Acts 2:1–13). In addition to brainstorming words to describe 'wind', the children thought about what wind could do.

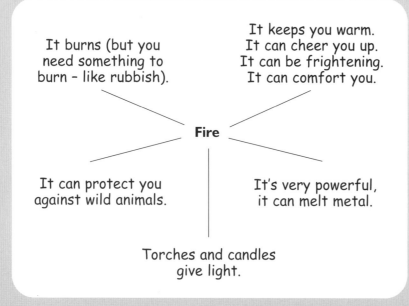

It burns (but you need something to burn – like rubbish).

It keeps you warm.
It can cheer you up.
It can be frightening.
It can comfort you.

Fire

It can protect you against wild animals.

It's very powerful, it can melt metal.

Torches and candles give light.

It can be strong or gentle.

You can see what it does (blows clouds, leaves...) but you can't see the wind itself.

Wind

It sails boats.
It's used for enjoyment.
It can keep gliders and kites up in the air.

It blows the propellers of wind turbines and that gives us power.

The teacher introduced the Hebrew word *ruach*, and explained how it had three meanings, 'wind', 'breath' and 'spirit', and that this word helped many people to understand better what God is like:

God is a strong force; can be strong or gentle.

God cannot be seen but His presence can be felt. It's a comforting presence, and a strengthening presence.

The teacher introduced the 'fire' images used by Christians:

God is an illuminating presence showing us* the way.

God gives protection and comfort.

God is powerful and can help people get rid of /burn the rubbish in their lives.

God can transform/change people.

Each of these ideas was discussed and then a class poem was written including much of what had been learnt.

---

* Whilst the words 'us' or 'we' may be appropriate in a Christian setting, in most schools it would be more appropriate to say 'Christians believe that ...' or 'Most Christians believe that ...'.

God is like the wind because:

He is all powerful,

He is the Breath of Life,

He is everywhere,

He is gentle like a breeze,

Like a hurricane He is strong.

We cannot see Him

But we know He is there.

We feel Him, we hear Him,

We see what He does.

Flowers swaying, water rippling,

Leaves rustling, waves tossing,

Windmills spinning, seas roaring.

Is it the wind or is it God?

The teacher told the children about the first Pentecost and was very careful to make clear that this story had been told many times before being written down, and that the use of picture language, i.e. using 'fire' and 'wind', made the account more vivid, and easier to remember. The children asked questions and were encouraged to think of possible answers. They were continually reminded of what 'fire' and 'wind' stood for.

Possible Follow-Up Work

This work could be followed by asking the children where they get their power, courage, determination from. This could be expressed in poetry or colour and design.

With **older children** more detailed work might be tackled: for example, an examination of the difference the coming of the Holy Spirit made in the lives of the followers of Jesus, as follows:

The teacher wrote up the two headings 'before Pentecost' and 'after Pentecost' on the board and the children recalled instances that would fit under each. After exhausting their ideas, the teacher added extra ones and referred to the biblical references.

THE DISCIPLES

before Pentecost	after Pentecost
• They were afraid; they barred the door because they were afraid of the Jewish authorities. (John 20:19)	They went out to meet the crowds. (Acts 2:5–14)
• They were sad; their master had been humiliated and put to death.	They were full of joy. (Acts 2:46, 47)
• They didn't understand their part in Jesus' work. They were learners, followers, disciples.	Now they knew what Jesus wanted them to do. (Acts 2:42–47) From being disciples they became apostles.

She then added:

The Holy Spirit had completely changed their lives, as fire does to metal or wind in a kite. The results may well be unpredictable!

Part of a class display showing images representing God's presence: the flames of fire; the dove descending – the baptism of Jesus (Mark 1:10).

This followed the work on the Resurrection, but it was felt necessary to refer briefly to the Ascension so that the children knew that Jesus was no longer visible to the disciples, but that before he left he made them a promise of the Holy Spirit (Acts 1:6–9).

The teacher began the lesson by asking the children if they would look any different if they were filled with power. Most answered, 'No'. She then asked:

If you wanted to show power filling someone, what colours might you use? What shapes might you use?

I want to read you a story about people being filled with power. Notice how the power is described.

She then read the account of the coming of the Holy Spirit as retold by J. G. Priestley in *Bible Stories for Classroom and Assembly: New Testament* (RMEP).

Power coming out of the ball, with streaks of powerful colours coming into the ball.   *Paul.*

The children were then asked:

What words would you use to describe this power that came into the lives of the disciples?
power   wisdom
Holy Spirit   courage
Christ be in you Pentecost

They were asked to express this sense of power through colour and shape, using pastels on A3 paper. As they drew and coloured the teacher walked round and wrote down some of the children's comments about the work they were doing.

Questions were used to conclude the lesson:

Do you think this story of Pentecost is important to Christians? Give reasons.

Have you ever felt empowered?
When you win something.
When I've earned something.
When it's a special time.
When you give something to someone.

Is this the same kind of empowerment the disciples experienced? Say why/why not.

It's like static electricity coming out of the man's body, and I'm going to do red on one half and yellow on the other to show strength and power.   *Douglas.*

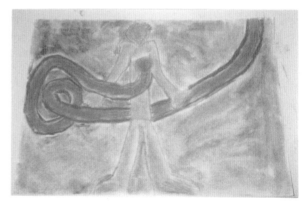

The power is going into him. It's going into his heart because that's where the will power is..... Well, in real life it's in your brain, but in Christianity it's in your heart.   *Robert.*

Pentecost 3: Peter after Pentecost

It was felt important that these children, who had already worked on the topic of Pentecost, knew not only that Christians believe that the disciples received the power of the Holy Spirit but what difference this power made in their lives. Peter was chosen as an example, and the accounts used were from Acts 3–4.

The lesson began with an exercise about themselves. Each child was given a square piece of paper, folded it in four and wrote their name in the centre. As each question was read out the children answered it on their sheet of paper.

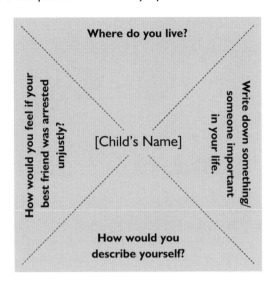

In sharing what they'd written, they discovered that whilst some children had written identical answers others had very different ones.

In a group on the carpeted area of the classroom the children recalled what they could remember about Peter prior to Pentecost:

He was a <u>fisherman</u>.
And a <u>follower of Jesus</u>.
He was <u>afraid</u>.
Why?
He didn't try to save Jesus from being arrested.
Yes, he followed at a distance. (Mark 14:54)
He <u>told lies</u> to save himself.
When?
In the courtyard when he said he didn't know Jesus. (Mark 14:66)
He was <u>unreliable</u>.
What do you mean?
He said he'd never leave Jesus but he did. (Mark 14:27)
All the disciples were afraid because when they met they locked the door. (John 20:10)
He got <u>upset</u> when the cock crowed because he went out and cried. (Mark 14:72)

The teacher continued:

> **Let's see what happened after Peter received the Holy Spirit at Pentecost.**

The teacher read the account of Acts 3–4 as told by J.G. Priestley in *Bible Stories for Classroom and Assembly: The New Testament* (RMEP), and then asked the children in what way Peter was different.

> He wasn't afraid any more.
> He had power and could heal people.

The children reflected further using a pyramid shape:

- On the central square they wrote about Peter before Pentecost.

- On the four outer triangles they wrote about Peter after Pentecost.

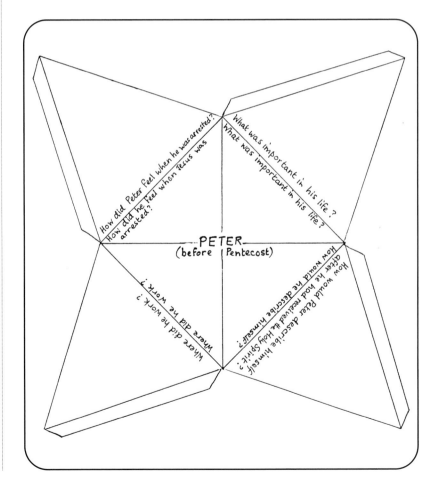

Here are some of their answers regarding Peter after Pentecost:

Important in Peter's life
The power he had
Preaching
Jesus' power
Jesus' work
The Holy Spirit in him
to stand up to other people

How might Peter have described himself?
brave-hearted
happy
fearless
confident
powerful
strong-hearted
courageous

Peter's feelings when arrested
no longer afraid
brave and angry
ready to start again

fearless and proud
alive, joyful
innocent

happy because he's done something Jesus wanted
relieved at not being arrested for something bad

When sharing their answers the children realized that though the answers were often very different they could all be true.

The children cut out their shapes, coloured them and made their pyramids.

The lesson ended with a discussion around the question:

Why do you think Pentecost is so important to Christians?
It helped the disciples carry on what Jesus started.
Yes it's the birthday of the Church.
It started other people believing.
Yes, up till then the real followers of Jesus had been his disciples and close friends, but now all kinds of people became followers.

I wonder why?

Possible Follow-Up Work

A discussion and possibly written work answering the question: 'Can you think of a time when you changed from feeling afraid to feeling and acting confidently? What made the difference?'

Prayer

Possible Learning Outcomes

This work on prayer (pages 59–63) is designed to help children to:

- understand what prayer is and why people pray, and that there are different kinds of prayer (AT1/2);

- know that prayer is an important part of the life of religious people (AT1);

- reflect on a selection of prayers that have meaning for them (AT2);

- express deeply held concerns through prayers or prose (AT2).

When teaching about prayer our objective is an educational one and doesn't assume commitment by those we teach. At the same time we want to make it meaningful to them and want to affirm those who do pray.

Prayer 1

By way of preparation the teacher had collected a considerable number of prayers which were attractively mounted. Some had been bought as cards, others came from books. One very useful source was Christopher Herbert's *Prayers for Children* (National Society, 1993).

The prayers were set out around the classroom and the children were asked to find one that had meaning for them. They were asked to forget that they were prayers and just to concentrate on the subject-matter. (The teacher felt this explanation was necessary as there were six self-confessed atheists in the class.)

Having chosen a prayer, each child was asked to:

- Copy out those lines that had the most meaning for them.
- Write down why they had chosen that prayer.
- State how they thought the writer of the prayer was feeling.

> **If his eyes had been guns**
> **we would all have been dead**
> **Lord, with your help my eyes**
> **will speak peace and not war.** *
>
> This prayer explains how God watches over us and how we can ask him for help to be friendly and not angry.
>
> It was written by somebody who had been experiencing hard looks and unkindness. This prayer gets you thinking.
>
> DAVID

> **Lord, make us instruments of Thy peace.**
> **Where there is hatred, let us sow love;**
> **Where there is injury, pardon;**
> **Where there is discord, union;**
> **Where there is doubt, faith;**
> **Where there is despair, hope;**
> **Where there is darkness, light;**
> **Where there is sadness, joy;**
> **For Thy mercy and Thy truth's sake.**
>
> **ST FRANCIS OF ASSISI**
>
> I chose this prayer because of the way he has used the words as well as the ideas. I think a person who cared would write this prayer. I think he would be feeling happy and rejoiceful to write words like these.
>
> KATIE

* From Hencher, J. & Herbert, C. *A Place to Dream*, copyright © 1976 Hereford Diocesan Council of Education.

This was followed by an opportunity for the children to read their prayers to the whole class and say why they'd chosen them. About half the class took part. During this time children began to recognize that there were different types of prayer.

A lengthy discussion followed around the questions:

Who prays?
Christians
People from different religions

Why do some people pray?
To thank God
To express their feelings to God
To show concern.

What do people pray about?
What they have done in the day
Asking for forgiveness
Thanking God
Asking for help for others

So what is prayer?

After a considerable silence one child said:
It's about things that are important to you.

The teacher asked the children to sit quietly, perhaps with their eyes closed to help them concentrate, and to think of something that was really important to them. After a minute's silence she asked them to write down what they had been thinking, either in the form of a prayer or as a piece of prose, or a poem. No-one complained or said they couldn't do it, and the results showed the depth of their thinking.

The prayers included the following:

> Dear God, please help all the people who are starving. Try to stop all wars and help crops to grow again. Stop people starving, please! The world would be so much better without starvation and wars. Please help us, God. We will help as much as we can if you tell us how.
>
> EMILY

(Here there is a realization that prayer isn't about foisting responsibility onto God, but working with God.)

> Dear Lord, please help to protect wild life and all living creatures on the earth, like the children who get killed by drunk drivers, and the animals that get crushed by cars.
>
> RUTH

> Dear Lord, help others to understand the meaning of your earth, how it works, how to share. We can only do this with your help, O Lord.

> Lord, thank you for all the enjoyment, all the fun we get from animals; but also, Lord, help us to understand them. Don't let us use them in ways that undermine them, ways that give only us pleasure. Help people to understand their needs.
>
> CHARLOTTE

The children who wished had an opportunity to share their prayers with the rest of the class, and then the teacher read:

> **Christ has no body now on earth but yours, no hands but yours, no feet but yours; yours are the eyes through which is to look out Christ's compassion to the world; yours are the feet with which he is to go about doing good, and yours are the hands with which he is to bless us now.**

She asked the class:

> **What do you think St Theresa meant when she said these words?**

The children who chose other forms of writing were equally moving:

> Hunger.
> The sad puzzled eyes of small starving children.
> No food to eat, no fresh water to drink.
> No future for them like we have.
>
> DANIELLE

> I think everybody should recycle a little. It doesn't pollute as much air, and saves money. You could recycle clothes. That would help the homeless and starving.
>
> JOANNE

> I think it's good to have friends that understand you and cheer you up when you feel sad and alone. My friends mean a lot to me, so I treat them how I would like to be treated.
>
> ASHLEY

> Trees
> breathe out oxygen.
> It gives us life.
> Don't forget to say
> Thank you.
>
> JOHN

The children who chose to write prose and poems also had an opportunity to read their work to the class. The lesson ended with a sharing of ideas regarding ways in which we can all help to care for our world.

Making Use of Children's Work in Class or School Worship

The children's prayers could be collected into a class book or file for use in worship. The prose and poems could also be included and used in times of reflection – 'quiet thinking time'.

The 'lesson' on prayer lasted nearly half a day, the teacher having decided that two weeks' RE be taken on one day.

As the children had entered into the work so readily, the following lesson was used to look at prayer in another world faith.

In the centre of the classroom a display was created of beautiful or interesting objects and photographs. The teacher explained that today they were going to look at a particular kind of Jewish prayer called 'Blessings'; that many blessings could be found in the Jewish service book, e.g.

Blessed are You, O Lord our God, King of the universe, who has kept us in life, and has preserved us, and has enabled us to reach this season.

This was a prayer that could be said on tasting any fruit for the first time in the season, or moving into a new house, or wearing a new garment for the first time. The children were quick to see that this prayer implied a constant awareness of God, and a constant attitude of thankfulness.

The opening words

Blessed are You, O Lord our God, King of the universe

were written on the board, and it was suggested that the children each chose an object from the display and wrote a blessing about it using these opening words. An example was given to them. Before choosing an object the children were asked to write

down the opening words. This ensured staggered choosing! Anyone who complained that 'their' object had been taken was encouraged to move their chair so that they could see the object clearly.

Blessed are You, O Lord our God, King of the universe, who gives us such brightly coloured dolls, that were made hundreds of miles away, yet we can still get pleasure from them here.

CHARLOTTE

Blessed are You, O Lord our God, King of the universe, who gives us beautiful animals and skilled craftsmen who may make models of them.

DAVID

Blessed are You, O Lord our God, King of the universe, who gives us men who have the skill to make interesting sculptures whith there bare hands.

JAMES

Having completed their blessings the children gathered round the display table, which had been cleared of all unused objects and photographs. Each child in turn placed their object back on the table and read their prayer. After a slight pause the next child followed suit until everyone had shared.

For some children it may well have been a time of prayer, for others just a sharing of something they had written; but for all, a sense of appreciation of what blessings are about. Everyone listened intently and there was a real sense of occasion.

Possible Follow Up Work

1. An excellent way to follow-up the writing of blessings would be to use the Jewish Hasidic practice of collecting '100 Blessings and Enjoying the Moment' to be found on page 93 of *Values and Visions: Spiritual Development and Global Awareness in the Primary School* (available from DEP, c/o Manchester Metropolitan University, 801 Wilmslow Road, Didsbury, Manchester M20 8RG; Tel. 0161 445 2495). Collecting a hundred blessings during the day is quite a reasonable task when shared among a whole class.

2. Discuss the importance of prayer in other world faiths, e.g. in Islam:

   - **Why do you think Muhammad (pbuh) said: 'Prayer is a refreshing stream into which you dip five times a day'?**

   - **Why do you think Muslims pray five times a day?**

   - **Why do many people think prayer is important?**

   - **What is really important in your life?**

Learning to Be Still

Children get more out of RE if they are able to sit at ease and be quite still, and reflect on the matter in hand. For many children this can be difficult unless they are taught certain techniques and are given opportunities to practise them. Many of the lessons recorded in this book use these techniques.

1. Being Alert and Relaxed

Use instructions like 'sit in an alert and relaxed position' at the beginning of every stilling exercise, so that the children know precisely what to do. It becomes part of the ritual.

(i) Turn your chair so that it's facing me and not touching your table/desk. Sit right back on your chair so that your back is right up against the back of your chair. Put both feet flat on the floor. [You may need to get smaller/higher chairs for some children, or put a box or some books under their feet.] Place your hands in a cup-like position in your lap, or let them lie loosely on your knees. Give your shoulders a shrug to make sure you're relaxed even though you're sitting upright. Now you're sitting in an alert and relaxed position.

With young children this can be made into a game:

(ii) 'Who can sit right back on their chairs with their feet flat on the floor? Stand up and when I say sit down see if you can sit like that.' …

While you're sitting in an alert and relaxed position see if you can let your eyelids close very gently … while I count 3 [then count 5 then 10].

A count of 3 is sufficient for young children to begin with. Again a game can be made out of closing eyes gently. 'Let's see if each group can close their eyes gently.'

(iii) I wonder whether we can breathe in for four and out for four, in and out through the nose.
In 2,3,4. Out 2,3,4.
Now breathe just as slowly by yourself without counting …

(iv) I wonder whether we can put all those things together? Can we sit alert and relaxed …With our eyes gently closed … and breathing slowly and gently … until I ask you to stop?

2. Breathing

Here are two possible ways.

(i) Sit in an alert and relaxed position … Let your eyes gently close … Now notice the way your breath enters and leaves your body … Listen to your breath … Begin counting each slow breath (in your mind). Each time you breathe in count one. When you've counted up to 4 breaths start again …

If your mind wanders, bring it back gently and start from one again … [Pause for a couple of minutes. With practice this time can be extended.]

Now be aware of the hardness of the chair you're sitting on … and when you are ready open your eyes … and have a good stretch …

(ii) **An exercise that will help children to experience stillness and the focussing of the mind.** The word 'tightening' may need to be discussed and demonstrated before you begin.

Sit in an alert and relaxed position with your eyes gently closed … Tighten your feet by curling your toes under … Hold them tense … now let them go … Tighten the muscles in your legs … hold them tight … now let them go (repeat this with) your bottom muscles … back … shoulders … hands – clenched … neck … face …

Your whole body has been tightened and now it is all relaxed … Now take a deep breath and breathe in whatever you need … it may be warmth, or comfort, or strength … With every breath breathe in whatever you need … [Longer pause]

Now be aware of the hardness of your chair … and when you're ready open your eyes and have a good stretch …

From: Stone, M.K. *Don't Just Do Something, Sit There.* RMEP.

10 and 11 year olds practise 'stilling', literally 'being still.'